Middle Management
in schools:
a survival guide

GW00507262

Middle Management in Schools
A Survival Guide

Richard Kemp
and
Marilyn Nathan

Blackwell Education

First published 1989

Published by
Basil Blackwell Ltd
108 Cowley Road
Oxford OX4 1JF
England

British Library Cataloguing in Publication Data

Kemp, Richard
Middle Management in Schools: a survival guide,
1. Great Britain. Secondary schools. Management
I. Title II. Nathan, Marilyn
373.12′00941

ISBN 0–631–17097–9
ISBN 0–631–16922–9 pbk

Typeset in 11/13pt Plantin
by Columns of Reading
Printed in Great Britain by Dotesios Ltd of Trowbridge

Contents

Chapter 1
Introduction

Who is this book for?

This book is an introduction to management for middle managers in schools.

In the past the middle management role in many schools was carried out largely by Heads of Department, whose function was to ensure the efficient delivery of a particular subject area in the school's curriculum – mathematics, art, physics or whatever. Under those circumstances the target group for this book would have been almost exclusively Heads of Department.

However, the number of middle managers in most schools has increased in recent years. This is partly a response to schools becoming larger, and partly in response to a range of new educational initiatives. There has been an expansion of pastoral middle management – Heads of Year, Heads of Sixth Form, Heads of Upper School etc. More schools are bringing a number of departments together as faculties, managed by a Head of Faculty. New initiatives, such as TVEI, are now managed by Co-ordinators. In fact we have now reached the situation in which there are relatively few members of a typical staff who do not have some form of middle management functions. It is for all these people that this book is intended.

In this book we try to provide the sort of information, advice and ideas you would find useful if you have, or are about to take on, one of the myriad of school middle management roles. The book tries to help you answer the question *What are my responsibilities as a middle manager, and how do I carry them out?*

We hope that three broad groups of middle managers will find the book useful:

1 *New managers* The book aims to provide extensive advice to newly-appointed managers. Some sections, such as Chapter 3 *How to get going*, are specifically geared to the needs of colleagues who have just been appointed to a middle management post.

2 *Aspiring managers* The book also aims to help those who are not yet managers but who would like to be. It will not tell you how to fill in your application form, but it will help you consider the questions and issues you might have to face as you progress towards, and into, middle management.

3 *Successful managers* One of the characteristics of a successful manager is that he or she never stops learning about management. So the book is also aimed just as much at those colleagues who want to update and develop their management skills further. Chapter 14, for example, suggests ways in which you can evaluate your work as a manager, something that you will want to do continuously.

We have tried to make the book 'user-friendly', by avoiding jargon where possible, and by offering practical advice which is based more on schools' and teachers' experiences than on a lot of academic management theory. However, we do feel that some theory is essential if you are to really understand your management role; where we have included management theory it is directly relevant to your task in school. Thus Chapter 8 examines management styles, and Chapter 9 touches on theories of team building as well as guiding you through practical activities.

Why do middle managers need a survival guide?

We have outlined what the book aims to do, but why do you, as an actual or potential school middle manager, need this sort of survival guide?

Your role has expanded and become more complex
You may need a survival guide because, as schools have become larger, not only has the number of middle managers in a school increased, but the volume and complexity of management tasks

has also significantly expanded. In the aftermath of the Education Reform Act this trend is certain to continue. As senior managers attempt to shoulder new burdens, one of their answers to management overload may be to delegate more and more of the school's management functions. In order to meet these new demands successfully you will need to develop your management skills.

> *The importance of leadership qualities and management skills has been documented in a number of recent HMI reports, and given impetus by the DES's current emphasis on management training for senior staff. However, although attention has mainly been focused on the senior management level, and on the formulation of school philosophies, policies, aims and objectives, it is at the departmental level that these are actually implemented. The head of department/middle manager plays a crucial role in the effective operation in the work of secondary school departments, requiring not only subject knowledge and teaching expertise, but also the ability to manage and lead a team.*
> (NFER, *Middle Management in Schools*, HoD Project)

The time when a Head of Department was simply the chief subject specialist, whose responsibility allowance was given largely for teaching the sixth form, is long gone. As the NFER extract above makes clear, the whole concept of middle management is expanding, and the responsibilities of middle management have increased as a result of the implementation of a range of educational initiatives, including Local Management of Schools and the National Curriculum. This is one reason why you might need a survival guide.

Lack of support elsewhere
Another reason why you might need a survival guide is that, although your responsibilities have expanded substantially, very little in the way of support and training is likely to be provided for you. The provision of middle management training varies enormously from one LEA to another. A few provide several levels of middle management training courses, ranging from foundation to advanced level. Many others provide no sort of training at all. On the whole, middle management training is a pretty hit and miss affair. Even where training does exist, the very

numbers of middle managers make it difficult for all those who want training to receive it.

Support and advice within individual schools varies enormously as well. In some it can be a question of sink or swim, while in others the support system for middle managers is clear-cut and effective. One difficulty is that, while the pastoral hierarchy in a school is often clearly defined, it is often far less clear to whom a department head or curriculum co-ordinator is immediately responsible. Thus, depending on the school, it can be difficult for middle managers to get advice and support.

Nor are there many books to which you can refer. There are certainly no handbooks or compendiums for the head of department or middle manager. This was one of the first things we discovered when we began to run middle management courses and course members asked us to recommend books. There are good books on specific issues, but nothing that seemed to meet all your needs as a middle manager in schools. Thus, in this book, we set out to provide the guidance and ideas which you may find difficult to obtain elsewhere.

How to use this book

In the book you will find practical advice about most of the tasks you face as a middle manager:

- What it means to be a manager
- How you start out
- How you deal with the administrative tasks a middle manager has to face
- How you should try to manage people, resources and time
- How you can build your team
- How you can provide staff development for your team members
- How to communicate effectively
- How to manage change
- How you can evaluate the work that you are doing

Integrated throughout the book are case study materials, which will give you the chance to consider, and work on, 'typical' school management issues. What we cannot give you is *the* management blueprint, for the simple reason that it does not exist. There is no 'right' way to manage. Our aim is to pose some key questions, and to outline some approaches and management strategies which you can consider and adapt to your own needs. The rest has to be up to you!

One approach to using this book would be to read it through from cover to cover. Alternatively you can dip into it for specific advice on an aspect of your management in which you feel you need information or support. However, if you are going to dip into the book, you will find it useful to know something about the way we have used case study material.

Case studies

All the chapters include case studies; they are numbered within each particular chapter. Many of the case studies, though not all, focus on an imaginary school called Bestwick Park, an urban, multi-cultural, mixed comprehensive. Even if your school is not urban, or multi-cultural, or even comprehensive, you will still find more than an echo of your own situation in the Bestwick Park case studies, and the issues outlined in the case studies generally will have a relevance to almost all school situations. You do not have to use the case studies sequentially, although you may find the school year has moved on somewhat since the last one you tackled.

There are three categories of case studies:

1 Exemplars
These are examples of how things are done, such as a sample job description, or an example of department meeting minutes.

2 For reflection
These case studies invite you to think about the issue raised, possibly linked to some discussion points.

3 For action
These case studies set out a situation, provide you with some information, and invite you to consider what action you would take – for example, by putting you in the place of a newly appointed Head of Science and asking you to determine your priorities for action in your first three weeks in school.

Chapter 2
What Does Being a Manager Involve?

Lovely person . . . brilliant teacher . . . wonderful with all sorts of kids . . . but utterly hopeless as Head of Department
(A teacher about her Head of Department)

But I'm a teacher not a manager. If I'd wanted to become a manager I would have gone into industry
(Interview answer of unsuccessful candidate for a HoD post)

The view expressed by the candidate above is fairly typical of people who still believe that education and management are incompatible; management is seen as something that happens in industry but not in education. We would argue that this view could hardly be further from the truth. All teachers are managers to some extent, and the management element of a teacher's role is going to increase in the future. As a teacher your management role is not the same as the management role of an engineer in ICI, or of a bank manager, or of a doctor, but a management role it certainly is. Any organisation or institution that has a particular purpose has to be managed, and a school is no exception. In order to achieve its aims a school has to have objectives; to achieve these objectives, the various people with responsibilities in the school have to plan, organise and lead.

In the running of a school clearly the Head and Deputies have the strongest management functions – they make up what many schools call the senior management team. Yet all the teachers in the school also have a management role to play in converting the school's educational aims into effective reality. In this the middle managers have a key role, a point which is emphasised in a wealth of research evidence.

Schools rely more for their success on the dynamism and leadership qualities of the Head of Department than on any other factor.

(DES Welsh Office Project)

Being a successful middle manager, whether Head of Department, Co-ordinator or Pastoral Team Leader, involves more than just being a good teacher. Someone can be an excellent classroom teacher, yet a poor middle manager. Your skill in the classroom may be what wins you the respect of other staff and contributes to your promotion, but you will need some new and different skills to succeed as a middle manager.

Who are the middle managers in a school?

There is no simple definition of middle management in schools. The closest one can come to a definition is to say that the school's middle managers are those people whose role places them between the senior management team and those colleagues whose job description does not extend beyond the normal teaching and pastoral functions. In practice the middle managers will be mainly those staff holdings posts of responsibility with an incentive allowance between A–E. However, because of the temporary nature of some A grade allowances, there will also be some staff on the main scale who are also carrying out middle management functions.

The diagram overleaf shows some typical middle management jobs, although it is by no means exhaustive.

In other words, middle managers are the people who have the day-to-day responsibility for managing departments or sections of the school, or for co-ordinating some form of activity or initiative (for example, TVEI or PSE), or for leading some form of staff team (for example, a year group).

What do we mean by management?

At this point it is worth thinking in more detail about what we mean by management. Every book written or course run is likely

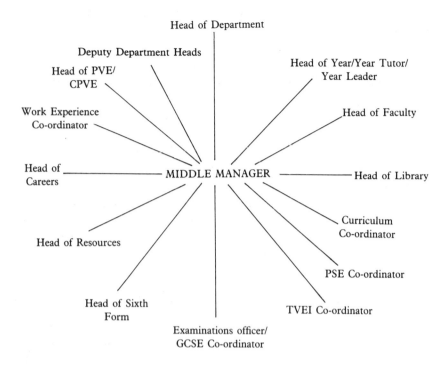

to provide a slightly different definition of 'management'. Four definitions are outlined below. Although they do differ somewhat, they are all closely related.

Management is . . .

- The setting of overall objectives, the formulation of policy and plans designed to achieve these objectives, and the establishment of standards for measuring the activity that puts people, money and machines to work in the production of goods and/or services.
- The planning and oversight of the activities of an organisation in relation to its goals, procedures and the tasks of its personnel.
- The name given to the totality of executive control, ie planning, co-ordination, leadership and evaluation.
- Getting things done through people, with the most effective use of all the available resources.

Whatever the form of words, two key elements emerge from these definitions:

1   To manage effectively you must have a clear idea of what you are trying to achieve
2   To be an effective manager you must be able to manage both *tasks* and *people*.

The definitions quoted above all derive from industry or commerce, yet the ideas apply just as much to education and schools.

Leadership

The terms 'leadership' and 'management' are sometimes confused, and this can be unhelpful when we are thinking about what being a manager involves. As a middle manager in a school your job may be described as 'leading a team of colleagues'. It might be less confusing if we rephrased this as '*managing the work* of a team of colleagues'.

To be a good manager you do not have to be a 'born leader', as the phrase goes. Certainly some people are very successful because they are charismatic leaders who can respond intuitively to people and situations. However, history is littered with as many cases of charismatic leaders who have not made good managers.

Middle management in schools does usually involve leading a team of colleagues, but 'leadership' in the sense of planning, co-ordinating and evaluating the work of the team as a whole. You do not have to be a born leader to be an effective manager. Almost all the skills required to be an effective manager can be learned, developed and improved. The question is thus whether one is prepared to go through the necessary learning process. Anyone can learn to manage better, though it requires effort, adaptability and practice.

Management for quality

The task of the middle manager in a school is highly complex and demanding. One of the common misconceptions about 'management' is that it is primarily concerned with efficiency. Of course it is important to be efficient, as efficiency is one (but only one) of the elements in being effective in what you are trying to achieve. But management in schools is much more than being efficient.

Education is about people – so is management. A school's purpose is to provide the best possible opportunities for the people in that school – pupils and staff. In other words managing a school is about providing *quality*. Management for quality is a key theme of this book.

Clear thinking – Seeing the wood for the trees

One of the most important attributes of a good manager is clear thinking – the ability to be able to stand back from a situation or problem and think clearly and calmly before deciding on a course of action. Whether your task is to make a long-term plan or to deal with an immediate crisis, to be effective you must have a *clear vision* of what you are trying to do, and *clarity of thought* when it comes to analysing how you are going to do it. In other words you have to be able to see the wood for the trees.

There are some ways of tackling problems and situations which can help you to think clearly about them. An approach to problem-solving is outlined in this chapter, linked to some case studies. In Chapter 13 we look at a task management model which can be used for managing change.

Meeting short and long-term objectives – Striking the right balance

One thing is for sure, as a middle manager you will find yourself

"Don't bother me with your ideas now, I've got a job to do."

dealing with 'problems' fairly frequently. Quite likely most of those problems will come up when you are in a rush trying to do something else!

It is easy to become snowed under by the immediate demands of the job, to find yourself in a situation where your time is spent *reacting* to events for most of the time. Two points need to be made here.

1 You will have to react to problems, so you will need an effective approach to *problem solving*.
2 You should try and strike a reasonable balance between the time you spend reacting to events, and the time you spend working on things you have initiated yourself, the things you as a manager think are important – your *proactive* role.

Certainly you will have to react effectively to many short-term problems, yet the longer-term success of your work may well depend on your being proactive by thinking and planning ahead. These two points – the need for clear thinking, and the need to balance your reactive and proactive roles – apply to all managerial situations. They are key themes throughout this book, which we hope you will bear in mind when you work on the case study material.

Case Study 2.1
STRIKING A BALANCE

*For
reflection*

The case of Nigel North, Head of Fourth Year, illustrates the need to strike the right balance between being reactive and proactive.

Nigel was always rushing around dealing with the day to day problems that are the lot of a head of year. He was under a lot of pressure – and a lot of stress. Every moment of his non-teaching time seemed to be taken up with his pastoral role – seeing pupils sent to him by other colleagues, dealing with requests for information about pupils, and so forth.

Matters came to a head when Nigel cancelled a half-termly

Tutor Team meeting, in order to supervise a detention for two pupils. The main item on the agenda of the Tutor Team meeting was to have been to discuss the Head's draft proposals for the introduction of a programme of personal and social education, to be taught by form tutors.

Nigel simply was not acting as a manager. He had got himself into a situation in which he was unable to think clearly about his priorities – to sec the wood for the trees. He was filling his days doing things that seemed urgent to him, and not doing the things that really were important for him to be doing as a middle manager.

An approach to problem-solving

As a manager dealing with problems is part of your day to day job. It is probably a good day which goes by without some sort of problem. Problems may be:

Personal	Pastoral or disciplinary
Departmental	Academic
Interdepartmental	Resources
School	Premises

Sorting out your priorities
You probably only have a limited amount of time – so it's important to establish your *priorities*. Two things affect the priority-rating of a problem:

How *urgent* is it?
How *important* is it?

The urgency of a problem will determine how quickly you deal with it, while the importance of a problem should affect how much time you are prepared to give it. Be ruthless with your time – don't waste it by spending too long on unimportant problems. Be ruthless with yourself, too – spend time dealing with things that are really important, not the things that are easier or more enjoyable.

Case Study 2.2   *For*
ESTABLISHING PRIORITIES   *reflection*

8.40 am, five minutes before morning registration . . . two
problems face you as Head of Year.

Problem A
Moira, the school secretary gives you a phone message from a
parent. It's about a school trip tomorrow. Do pupils have to wear
school uniform? Moira says that the parent sounded rather
agitated about things.

Problem B
A fairly unimportant query from a head of department seems to
indicate that one of your form tutors is clearly not following the
procedure you all agreed at the last Year Meeting as far as
following up pupil absences goes.

Problem B is clearly the more important issue.
Yet Problem A is the more urgent.
So deal with A first, but do not spend too long on it. Perhaps ask
Moira if she can spare a moment to ring the parent to give him the
information that he needs – no uniform is needed. If he still wants
to speak to you Moira will say that you will phone him back later
in the day – with luck Moira's message will deal with the problem.
   Problem B needs more thought and time. Don't rush into trying
to deal with it too hastily or without enough time, if necessary, to
talk it through with the tutor concerned.

Making problems more manageable – an approach to problem solving

This chapter has emphasised that the effective manager has clarity
of thought, and the skill to balance time spent on reacting to
problems with the time spent on working on the real priorities of
the job. Both these attributes are key elements in the approach to
problem solving outlined in Figure 2a below. The essence of this
approach, which is widely used, is that you should tackle a

problem in clearly-defined stages. Do not jump in trying to find solutions to a problem before you have clarified what the problem involves, and what your possible avenues for action might be.

This problem-solving approach is a technique that you can adapt and use in many of the aspects of your job as a middle manager. As a manager, your role involves making decisions all the time, whether they relate to short-term 'problems' or to ideas and strategies for tackling longer-term development priorities.

The three case studies that follow each outline a 'problem' situation. The first two show how the problem-solving approach could be used to clarify the issues involved – something we all

1 Clarification

- What is the problem?
- Does it have component parts?
- What are the current symptoms?

2 Analysis

- Diagnose the problem
- Categorise the symptoms
- Suggest possible causes
- Consider the viewpoints of different people concerned

3 Approaches

- Generate ideas for solution
- What are the possible strategies?
- Who can help with solution?

4 Action

- What can be done – in the short term and longer term?
- Specify steps to deal with problem
- Who is going to monitor progress?

Figure 2a: A problem-solving approach

need to do before going on to generate ideas for possible courses of action. The third case study presents a problem situation free of our comments, which gives you the opportunity to use the problem-solving approach from scratch. We hope that the approach will help you in making good decisions – both when you consider the studies in this book and, more importantly, in carrying out your management job in school.

Case Study 2.3   *For*
UNABLE TO ADJUST TO A CHANGE OF ROLE *reflection*

Yvonne Perkins, as Deputy Head, finds that a lot of staff consult her about professional issues. This is a conversation she had with Frances Marshall, Second in the Modern Languages department.

'We were all thrilled when Roger was appointed. He was so good with the children in the classroom, always doing exciting projects and producing such good work. His lessons gave the impression of being so well organised that we thought he would be a really good person to be Head of Department. I wanted him to get the job, even though I've been here longer than him and there were several good outside candidates. In fact the whole department was pleased. We all had such high hopes.

But it's been almost two years now, and things have gone from bad to worse. He just hasn't adjusted to being Head of Department. Either that or he simply hasn't got what it takes. I suppose he has routines, but I am not at all sure what they are. I don't know where anything is anymore. It's not just me either. I think you know that we all feel the same way. He doesn't seem interested in any of us, or what we are trying to do. He's out of school a great deal – on that GCSE materials project. The atmosphere in the department is getting really bad. People are becoming very slack about things. It's particularly hard for me because I'm second in department, so people turn to me all the time. Do I do his job for him or what?'

1   *What exactly is the issue here?*
2   *Does the issue have a number of component parts?*

The issue is that Frances, and possibly other members of the department have lost confidence in Roger as Head of Department.

The issue has a number of component parts:
- Poor management of the department's resources
- As second in department Frances is not sure of her role
- The work of department members is not being properly managed
- The department is not working together as a team

Case Study 2.4 *For*
A PROBLEM OF MANAGEMENT OVERLOAD *reflection*

Simon Tucker, Head of the Science Faculty, talks to Deputy Head Yvonne Perkins. It is about Chris Jones, the Head of Biology. Simon has had a note from Chris.

'I am finding things rather difficult at the moment, and would like to talk the situation through with you.

After two years here as Head of Biology I ought to be on top of things, but it doesn't seem to be working out like that. Within the department I am having to spend a lot of time supporting Mabel, helping her prepare her lessons and dealing with the problems that arise from them. Although Nigel is second in department, I know that he is so preoccupied with his duties as Head of Year, that I don't like to ask him to help out, so in fact I get no real help from him either in departmental administration or curriculum development. There is also the A level fieldtrip to Wales, the 4th year coursework visits and the greenhouse project which is nearing completion. More than that, I like to take a real part in the school's activities. I feel that it helps me as a Head of Department, and I enjoy working with pupils and colleagues outside the classroom. At the moment I am working with my tutor group preparing a stall for the school summer fete, I am involved with the minibus project and I shall be taking a group of pupils to France for 10 days at the end of term. Now Peter Greenwood, who is coming to France with me, has asked me to help him with the new school drama production. I'd like to help, but my wife is saying that I'm working too hard and that I have no time for her and the kids. I know that I'm often rather tired in the evenings, and I do get a bit irritable with the kids at times. Generally things seem to be getting on top of me a bit, and I would welcome having the chance to talk things through with you.'

1 *Clarification*
What is the problem?
Chris feels that he is not coping with the demands of his Head of Department job.
Does the problem have component parts?
- He does not seem to be getting much departmental support from Nigel.
- He feels he has to spend a lot of time supporting Mabel.
- He has taken on a heavy workload of extra-department activities.

What are the symptoms?
- Chris is clearly under stress, and this is affecting home life.
- Chris also clearly feels alarm at the mounting pressure of things he is committed to do at school.

2 *Analysis*
Chris
- Is Chris trying to do too much? If so, is this a short term or longer term issue?
- Has Chris really sorted out his priorities for his work at school? Has he sorted out his priorities between home and school commitments?
- Is one of Chris's problems that he finds it difficult to say 'No'? Can Chris delegate? Has he tried to share out department tasks?

Others involved
- Does Mabel really need the level of support Chris gives her?
- Is Nigel aware that Chris feels he is not pulling his weight in the department?
- Do people who ask Chris to do things (Peter and his play for example) realise the work pressure Chris is under?

3 *Approaches*
- Chris can be helped to sort out his priorities – in the

department, and for extra-department activities.

- Chris can be encouraged to have a planning session with Nigel, with aim of sorting out department priorities and workload.
- Can someone else be involved with supporting Mabel? Simon perhaps, or possibly Nigel.

4   Action

- Clearly there is no one straightforward solution to this problem. However, the central issue is that Chris must sort out his priorities as his current stress is related to feeling over-committed.
- He must reduce his extra-department load of activities – most he is already committed to, but he can say a regretful 'No' to Peter's play.
- Within the department, as an immediate action, he should be helped to sort out priorities. As a longer term action he can be helped to develop ways of involving others more fully in the running of the department.

Action plan

The immediate step is that Chris needs to talk through his situation with someone who understands the issues involved, and who is in a position to advise him on the actions outlined above – in effect Chris needs one or more counselling sessions. Yvonne is probably the person to do this most effectively. However, as Chris went to Simon initially, it is Simon who should talk to Chris first, and suggest that he goes to Yvonne to talk through the problem.

Subsequent actions will depend to some extent on the outcome of Chris's talk with Yvonne. Ultimately, however, it will be up to Chris to prioritise his time, and stick to his priorities.

Case Study 2.5   *For action*
A PERSON MANAGEMENT PROBLEM

Here is another situation relating to a new Head of Department. Once again Yvonne Perkins has been approached, this time by

Fiona Bruce, who was appointed Head of English just over six months ago.

'I heard that Vera wanted the post very badly, and had expected to get it, so I wasn't too worried when she wasn't very welcoming when I first arrived. I thought that this was a situation I was mature enough to cope with, and that if I treated her reasonably we would both be professional enough to ride it out. After all it happens often enough.

But it hasn't improved at all, and in fact at times it has been very difficult indeed. She has a very cutting tongue and cannot resist sniping at me, particulary at department meetings, where she not only belittles everything I suggest, but regularly tries to create the impression that perfectly normal procedures are new and quite unreasonable demands on my team. Sometimes this means that it is very difficult for me to get them to co-operate.

What's more she is doing so little. I'm told that in the past she practically ran the department. Well, now it is more like having a part-timer! I cannot depend on her doing anything I request. She is regularly late, and as you know, quite often absent, and I feel this is having an effect on the whole department. Certainly the absence rate in the department is much higher than in my previous school. It is wearing on my nerves as well as being very divisive, and it is having such a bad effect on department morale . . .'

Use the approach to problem-solving outlined in this chapter to suggest an approach to solving this problem.

Chapter 3
How to Get Going

The outgoing Head of Department had asked me to tea at her home to meet the department. Unfortunately I had not worked out how long it would take me to get there from my own school. I was late and they had to wait for over an hour. They looked at me as if they had already decided that I was totally disorganised and quite incapable of running a department. I felt awful. In fact the experience undermined my confidence in dealing with the department for a long time . . .

I was nervous before I started at my new school, but I expected that. Yet I was also confident that I could do the job. I'd been teaching for some years, and I had been closely involved with running the department at my old school. What I had not realised was how quickly the demands would pile in on me; I suppose I had thought that I would have time to play myself in as it were. In fact I found that I had to make some quite important decisions almost immediately; I had to decide on which text books to order within that first week, as the previous person had not wanted to make decisions for me. The silly thing is that I would have had plenty of time to do some of these things over the summer before term started. If I had been better prepared I don't think I would have felt so overwhelmed in that first half term . . .

Congratulations, we would like to offer you the post . . . Being organised right from the start is important. Certainly first impressions count for a lot. Once you have succeeded at interview and have been appointed to your Head of Department or other middle management post, you want to get off to the best possible start – it is important both for your own confidence, and for the impression you make on your colleagues.

This chapter looks at some things you will need to do before, or soon after, taking up a new middle management post. The advice is intended primarily for middle managers who are taking up post in a new school, but some of the points apply just as much to people who are promoted within their existing school.

Ten steps to getting started

1 *Make some time to plan and prepare*
Usually you will have at least part of a term between being appointed and taking up your new post. Put aside time during this period to prepare yourself. Time spent in planning and preparation almost always pays dividends.

Some planning work can be done in the holidays before you start, but some things need to be done before the end of the previous term – so get yourself organised in time.

2 *Brief yourself as fully as possible*
a) *About the LEA*. Each LEA largely determines its own procedures and policies. You may find that moving just a few miles over an LEA boundary into a new authority means that you have to cope with a system very different from the one to which you are accustomed. Find out how the LEA is organised, and whether it has any particular policies or priorities which could affect how you do your management job.

b) *About the school*. Provide yourself with enough basic information about your new school to enable you to cope with the first few days of term – the time when you will be particularly anxious to look and sound as if you know what you are doing and where you are going! How is the school organised? What is the school layout? Who are the key people? Does the school have any particular policies or priorities which could affect the way you do your job?

c) *About the department or team*. Nobody expects you to know everything about your new department before you start, indeed, you don't want to prejudge things. But you do need to find out some basic information about the curriculum and the way it is taught, about the way the department is currently organised, and whether there has been a particular philosophy or approach which could affect how you approach your management role.

Make a list of all the things you feel you need to find out about before the end of the term prior to taking up your post.

3   *Send for information*
Send for any available brochures and leaflets. A phone call to the Education Office should produce some information about the LEA. The school secretary should be able to send you a staff handbook, parent brochures, and other relevant documents. It is well worth reading these before you visit the school again. The staff handbook may be a valuable source of information about procedures, people and philosophy.

4   *Visit the school*
Visit the school again if this is at all possible. If you have not been invited to do so, then ring up and ask if you can come in at a convenient time before the end of term. This will give you the chance to meet people (away from the rather artificial circum-

Send for information

stances of the interview), to collect your timetable and other material you might need to prepare your courses. You can also pick up any further items or information that the school had not thought to send you. The day will give you the chance to be clear about what happens on that first day of term. Are you, for example, expected to run a department meeting?

5 *Meet your department or team*
If possible, give all the members of the department the chance to meet you for a brief informal chat before the start of the new term – do not forget the part-timers as well. It is so much easier to get off to a smooth start if you and the rest of your team are not complete strangers.

The rest of the department will have a perfectly natural curiosity about you, and your willingness to spend a little time talking to them individually will help to create a good initial impression. Make sure that you do not miss anybody out – a sure way to risk ill-feeling!

Even if you have been promoted within your existing school, then it is still a wise (and tactful) move to have a short individual talk with each member of the team before taking post. It can reassure people and ease the transition.

6 *Spend time with the outgoing Head of Department*
When you visit the school, make sure that you have the opportunity for a long talk with your predecessor. You are not, of course, committed to continuing his or her policies, but you do want as much inside information about the department as possible, and the previous Head is likely to be the best source. She or he is likely also to appreciate you wanting to consult him or her – and remember, she or he may still be a very influential person with the rest of the team. Make sure that you receive copies of all the department documents, resource lists, accounts etc.

7 *Clarify what is expected of you*
You need to be clear right from the start about what is expected of you as a Head of Department or Team Leader in that particular school. It is a useful, and professional, move to book an appointment with the Head or Deputy in order to discuss your role in the school. You should have received a written job description which will form a basis for this discussion. If you have

not been given a job description, ask for one now – you do not want to discover anything quite unexpected when you arrive to take up post!

8   *Walk the course*

Some time spent simply wandering around the school can be very useful. It's worth going in a day or so before terms start to do this (you may want a time when the students are not around – the calm before the storm!). Life is so much easier if you are familiar with the layout of the place before you have to start dealing with students as well. Make sure that you have a plan of the buildings and rooms.

This is also a good time to pop in to meet the school secretary and the office staff, to thank them for sending you the information about the school. The office is very important to the life of the school, and you will need its support. Other people it might be useful to meet are the caretakers and reprographics technicians – you are likely to be highly dependent on their goodwill over the years!

You will particularly want to investigate further the facilities of your own department or area. Where are things located? What state are things in? You may be itching to sort things out a bit, but be careful, you may not yet be in a position to judge just what you need or want to keep.

9   *Think through your priorities*

In the previous chapter we suggested that there are two factors which determine the priority rating of a problem or issue:

- How *urgent* is it?
- How *important* is it?

Urgent problems are the things which need to be dealt with *now*, so that the smooth running of the department will not be affected during the takeover period. There are some decisions which may have to be taken almost immediately. These may be merely routine matters. Some may be things which your predecessor, intentionally or unintentionally, left to you. Anything in this 'urgent' category must be sorted out, preferably before the start of term – it really is important to clear away these urgent tasks effectively.

Investigate the facilities of your department.

Once that has been done you can begin the process of determining your priorities. You can use the information you have assembled to begin to assess the current state of the department, to evaluate its strengths and weaknesses, and to begin to sort out your possible short-term and long-term priorities for action. You are likely to want to make a proper analysis of your department or area of responsibility early on in your first term – this may be one of your most important short-term priorities. Some guidelines for doing this are outlined later in this chapter.

10 *Make your mark – sensitively*
It is important for you to make an impact on your team colleagues right from the start. Contrary to popular advice from some quarters, we would suggest that a dramatic gesture is probably inappropriate; nor is saying 'NO' to the first three requests from the department usually the best way of establishing your authority.

If you feel that you do want to make a gesture, try improving the appearance of the department's teaching rooms if you can do this without either involving other people in too much effort or risking treading on other people's toes.

What you really want is to demonstrate that you can do the job right from the start; that you have prepared yourself for the post; that you have given proper thought to things; that you are willing to consult people and to listen to their views and ideas; that you can administer, organise and make the necessary decisions. If you can do all this right from the beginning, then you will have made an immediate impact.

Finally, a short list of don'ts . . .

Don't feel you have to do everything on Day 1.

You don't have to change the world before half-term.

Don't do things without consulting your colleagues and talking things through with them.

Don't hide yourself away – be around for people to talk to.

Don't start with the idea that your first task has to be to 'establish your authority' (whatever that means).

Don't only be reactive – try and show some initiative too.

Analysing your role

In the '10 Steps' outlined above we suggested that it was essential to establish what is expected of you as a middle manager in your particular school. If at all possible you should try and do this before you actually start your job, so that you have a clear idea of your post as a whole, rather than a piecemeal notion of what you need to do. Once you get going you will certainly find yourself facing numerous, and sometimes conflicting, demands. This initial overview can be crucial in helping you cope with them.

Your job description

This is the first thing to look at. It is now obligatory for all teachers to have a job description, so you should have been given one. The job description is a guide to how the role of Head of Department (or other middle management roles) is viewed in your

"Don't do things without consulting your colleagues first ."

school. It should indicate what is expected of you, and in what areas the school places its priorities (see Case Study 3.1).

Case Study 3.1   *Exemplar*
JOB DESCRIPTION OVERKILL

This is the job description for a Head of Department at Bestwick Park.

Bestwick Park High School – Head of Department

The Head of Department carries out a crucial middle management role. The number of responsibilities listed below indicates the importance of the post to the sound running of the school. The Head of Department's most essential tasks are to provide clear leadership for the staff teaching in his/her department and to act as a responsive and responsible 'middleman' between the Head and her/his senior colleagues and the teachers in his/her department. It is important also that the leadership of a department be exercised with a due regard for the overall objectives of the school.

The Head of Department's responsibilities include:

General
a) As a senior member of staff, to uphold standards and agreed school policy.
b) To provide leadership within the school community as a whole.
c) To attend school policy making meetings and be involved in the development of school curriculum in consultation with the Head and other senior staff.

Organisation, Administration and Staff Development
a) To establish departmental aims, objectives in accordance with the school's overall aims, with particular emphasis on equal opportunities and multi-cultural education.
b) To formulate and implement departmental policy within the agreed framework of school policy.
c) To prepare departmental timetable within the school TT framework.
d) To deploy staff and teaching groups in consultation with the Head and Deputy Head.
e) To prepare and make available to departmental staff adequate schemes of work which include:
   • clear aims and objectives
   • guidance on teaching methods and approaches
   • contents of the course, skills, concepts and knowledge
   • methods and frequency of assessment
   • homework
f) To be responsible for standards of work in the subject(s) covered by the department. This will involve ensuring and monitoring the proper planning, preparation, teaching and assessment of work within an agreed departmental policy, including regular setting and marking of homework.
g) To ensure that the curriculum within the subject reflects the

nature and the composition of the community within and outside the school.

h) To draw up a departmental responsibility structure with job descriptions wherever necessary.

i) To be responsible for the preparation, circulation and a constant review of the syllabus.

j) To be responsible for establishing a uniform procedure for continuous assessment of skills in the lower school in line with the criteria provided by the GCSE scheme.

k) To be responsible for the arrangements of the external and internal examinations.

l) To keep a record of and monitor external examination results within the department and to take necessary steps to improve them.

m) To be responsible for departmental budget and ordering and issuing of departmental stock. This involves keeping an up-to-date record of expenditure in a stock book to be checked by DH.

n) To be responsible for the maintenance in good order and security of departmental teaching rooms, equipment and stock. Generally making sure that departmental teaching areas present a lively and conducive atmosphere for learning.

o) To liaise with the Librarian, Head of Learning Support and other support and resource agencies within the school to ensure proper and full departmental use of the facilities available.

p) To deal with staff problems.

q) To liaise and maintain contacts with outside educational institutions such as primary schools, examination boards etc.

r) To arrange 'cover' work for absent staff. To provide work and support for the staff in charge.

s) To be responsible for advice, support and professional development of the members of department.

t) To ensure that the departmental team keep abreast of current developments in education in general, and their own subject area in particular.

u) To hold regular departmental meetings as a main line of communication. (Minutes to Headteacher.)

v) To conduct an annual review of the department with the Headteacher.

Pastoral

a) To be responsible for discipline and welfare within the department. To liaise with Heads of Year and DH (P) with regards to individual problems – personal or disciplinary.

b) To be responsible for the timetable, training and induction of student teachers and probationary staff.

c) To encourage and promote regular extra-curricular activities within the department.

This is a not untypical job description. It certainly tells us what the Head expects a Head of Department to do. The problem is that, as well as the introductory paragraph, there are 28 different items. Does the Head expect you to do all of them at the same time? Are they all equally important?

There is no way of knowing. It is almost as if the Head of Bestwick Park, in her desire to spell everything out for you, has lost sight of the wood for the trees. The job description loses sight of the fact that some tasks will be more important for the school or department than others, and that some tasks will be considerably more time-consuming than others. At first sight, therefore, rather than providing guidelines, such a document is likely to confuse and make you feel distinctly inadequate!

If you find yourself faced with a lengthy or unstructured job description, see if you can get hold of job descriptions for similar jobs in other schools. This should help you to identify what are the common elements to the job, and what elements are peculiar to your school.

Divide your job into main areas of responsibility

It helps to divide a lengthy job description into something more manageable. There are a number of ways you could subdivide your responsibilities. One good approach is to use the five areas recently identified by HMI as being the common areas of Head of Department responsibility:

> *The Head of Department plays a crucial role in the effective operation of the work of secondary school departments, requiring not only subject knowledge and teaching expertise, but also the*

ability to manage and lead a team (NFER). The Head of Department will have responsibility for implementing most of the school's philosophies, policies, aims, and objectives. The main areas of responsibility include:

- *Routine administration and organisation of the department*
- *The planning of pupils' learning experiences*
- *Monitoring and evaluating the work of the department*
- *Professional development within the department*
- *Liaison with other departments, with the pastoral staff, the senior management, and with outside agencies*

Go back to the Bestwick Park job description (Case Study 3.1) with its 28 items (or the job description given to you by the school), and see how many of the tasks you can fit under each of the five headings outlined by HMI above. This would be one way of structuring or shaping your own job description. Once you have done this you can use it as a basis for an agreement with your Head.

Making a departmental analysis

You may decide that one of your first priorities is to make a thorough analysis of the current situation of the department or area for which you are taking responsibility. You will probably need to do this before you can properly consider your longer-term priorities for action.

To do the analysis you will need copies of all the departmental documents – syllabuses, resource lists, job descriptions, examples of worksheets etc. You will also need to make time to talk to a range of people about the department – both those on the inside and those on the outside. It can be a good idea to ask different people the same questions about the department, and then to compare the answers you receive – this can help in distinguishing the rhetoric from the reality!

The aim of collecting all this information is to help you understand how the department functions, to determine what kind of work is done and by whom. This analysis of the state of the department as it is now is an important first step. It will help you to determine your short-term and long-term priorities.

Outlined below are some guidelines for making a departmental analysis. Any list of questions we give here cannot hope to be comprehensive, as each department will have its idiosyncrasies and special situations. The guidelines are intended merely as a starting point for you to make a list of questions that can form the basis of your own departmental analysis.

Guidelines for making a departmental analysis

1 *Syllabus*
- Is there a written syllabus? Is it easily available?
- When were any parts of it last evaluated/reviewed?
- Who was involved in this process?

2 *Resources*
- Is the department well resourced? (ie teaching rooms, AV equipment, stock, stationery)
- Are the resources catalogued?
- To what extent are the resources used?
- Where are resources stored? How accessible are they?
- Who is responsible for their maintenance?

3 *Capitation*
- What is the department's capitation? How does it fit into the school's capitation policy?
- What limits are there on your powers of spending?
- To what extent is spending delegated to members of the department?
- What is the current balance?

4 *Teaching*
- Are the pupils streamed, setted or taught in mixed-ability groups?
- Is this on the basis of school or departmental policy?
- How are departmental staff allocated to teaching groups?
- What variety of teaching and learning styles are commonly in use?
- Is there a school/department policy on homework and marking?
- What are the department's external exam results like? How do they compare with the school's results as a whole?

5 *People in the department*
- How long have colleagues been in the department? How does the pattern of staff turnover compare with that of the school as a whole?
- How do members of the department inter-relate? Is there much teamwork or cooperation?
- How would you assess the current mood of the department – contented, complacent, frustrated, apprehensive, confident . . .?

6 *Management*
- To what management style is the department accustomed?
- What has been the normal process of decision-making in the department?
- What has been the pattern of department meetings?

Chapter 4
Dealing with Administration

I didn't realise just how much paperwork there would be when I became a Head of Department. You seem to lose all the fun of teaching, and get bogged down in a lot of boring administration.

(Newly appointed HoD)

The new Head of Department quoted above had enjoyed being a subject teacher, and had quickly gained promotion. Now she felt burdened with a lot of what she considered 'clerical' tasks. These were taking up the time that could have been spent on things that, to her mind, were more important, such as lesson preparation, marking, and dealing with pupils.

This way of thinking indicates that she has not yet adapted to her changed role, and is still thinking as a classroom teacher and not as a manager. The job of Head of Department involves managing the operation of that department, and this inevitably means carrying out a range of administrative tasks. The difficulty for the middle manager in school is that he or she is one of the few managers who has to spend most of their working time doing something else – teaching pupils. Having only a limited time for administrative tasks means that it is vital to be clear about priorities and approaches to this part of the job. The administration, and the paperwork that often goes with it, needs to be viewed *as a means to an end*, and not as an end in itself. Being an efficient administrator helps the department to be good at its most important job – providing top quality teaching for children.

Thus administration is more than just 'paperwork'. As a middle manager your administration tasks will fall mainly into three categories:

1 The day-to-day tasks associated with your team's normal work, for example:
   - making sure that the necessary teaching resources are available in the right place
   - checking that work has been left by an absent colleague
   - making sure that GCSE coursework marks are being properly entered on record sheets

2 Organising and administering the department's contribution to occasional school events and activities, for example:
   - school exams
   - open days and parents' evenings
   - fieldtrips, visits

3 Dealing with all the paper that finds its way into your pigeon hole or on to your desk; in this task you are essentially reacting to things that come your way.

Good organisation and administration of your department or team is one of the keys to success as a middle manager, because it is the management skill which facilitates everything else that you do. To be a good administrator means that you have successfully managed *time, resources, communications* and *people*. This will certainly improve, rather than detract from, the learning opportunities for the pupils.

> *The HoD must first be an efficient administrator . . . a chaotic stock cupboard should not be regarded as a charming eccentricity but as industrial wasting of precious time and patience for all who have to grapple with it . . .*
>
> *Properly defined routines for all the potentially time-consuming activities of the department are an essential part of departmental organisation. Well-thought-out patterns can not only build up a unique and invaluable facility for the department, but strengthen the sense of working together, and release staff energies for tackling the multitude of other tasks that await.*
>
> D. Bennett and R. Edwards, *Schools in Action*
> (DES Welsh Office Project, 1985)

Ten pointers on how to be an effective administrator are outlined below. At the end of this chapter there are four case studies (4.2–4.5) designated '*For action*' which give you the chance to put some of these ideas into practice.

How to be an effective administrator – ten pointers

1   *Plan ahead*
The administrative load is always greatest at certain times of the year. If you organise your time well and plan ahead you can avoid falling into last-minute crisis management. Spend some time studying the school calendar, which most schools produce annually, so that you can work out when the busy times will be, and plan your work accordingly.

A year planner can be a useful organising tool. Write the important dates and deadlines on the year planner and keep it visible on your office wall (if you are lucky enough to have an office!). Alternatively, you could set out the same information as a flow chart in your diary. Both techniques will help you to anticipate the times when you know your work load will be heavy – exams, reports, capitation bids, ordering etc.

2   *Prioritise*
An effective manager always has a clear idea about the priorities for his or her work. For most of us there always seems to be a mountain of things that need doing. When you face such a mountain, ask yourself:

- What are the *most important* things?
- What are the *most urgent* things?

Some things will have a high priority because they are urgent; however, they may not be very important, and so can be done quickly without taking up too much time. Other things may have a high priority because they are more important; some important tasks may not have an urgent deadline, but to do them properly, and without a last-minute crisis, you need to make enough time for them now.

3   *Action plan*
Once you are clear about your priorities it is useful to plan *when* you are going to do things. Time is always short, so make an action plan. For most people a week is the most convenient time-span for action planning. A weekly action planning sheet can be useful (see Case Study 4.1). If and when additional tasks come your way during the week, determine their priority in relation to what you already have planned to do, and where necessary adjust your action plan accordingly.

  Remember: do high priority jobs first, then those that you really do not have time for will be the least important tasks.

4   *Make the time you need*
One of the difficulties of being a middle manager in school is that many of your management tasks have to be fitted around the time you spend teaching. This puts a premium on using the time you do have effectively. Your weekly action plan can help with this. Try and make a regular time slot for dealing with routine matters; for example, 30 minutes at the start of each day is usually enough to deal with anything in your pigeon hole.

  Be realistic in estimating the time you will need for tasks. Allow enough time to do the really important jobs properly. If necessary, put a limit on the amount of time you can afford to give to tasks which, for this particular week, have a lower priority rating. Attempting less and concentrating on top priorities can increase your productivity and effectiveness.

  Be ruthless with yourself about making good use of your time. 'I can never really do any work in school time' is a remark we quite often hear. 'Nonsense', is the short answer! Of course, if you choose not to use 'free' time during the school day and work at home during the evenings, that's up to you – but it is neither an effective nor a professional use of your time. Similarly, do not get distracted by minor, or more enjoyable, tasks when you have planned to do something more important. Case study 4.2 (page 42) gives you a chance to try out the decision rules outlined in Figure 4a, overleaf.

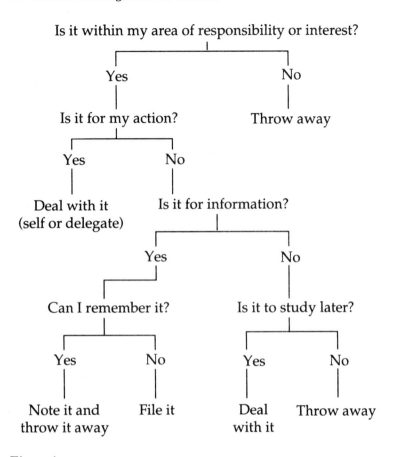

Is it within my area of responsibility or interest?

Yes — Is it for my action?

No — Throw away

Is it for my action?
Yes — Deal with it (self or delegate)
No — Is it for information?

Is it for information?
Yes — Can I remember it?
No — Is it to study later?

Can I remember it?
Yes — Note it and throw it away
No — File it

Is it to study later?
Yes — Deal with it
No — Throw away

Figure 4a
From: *Management in School Science Departments*, ASE/British Gas

5   *Disciplined decision making*

Bits of paper of various sorts will constantly make their way to your pigeon hole or desk. Your aim should be to handle each bit of paper *only once*. Make a decision on every bit of paper that crosses your desk or enters your pigeon hole, even if it is only a decision to seek advice, or decide when you can take action. This may be easier said than done, but try to discipline yourself to take action on a piece of paper the first time it comes into your hands. The path outlined in Figure 4a may help.

Do not put off to tomorrow what you can do today. The first Duke of Wellington had a dictum that one should always do the business of the day *in* the day. Sound advice, especially in the light of evidence that the average manager delays action on 60% of all the

Case study 4.1 *Example*

A WEEKLY PLANNER

[handwritten margin note: Talk to James – field course]

WEEK Priorities		
① 4th Year Assessments – mark		
② Resources for 5 Tourism Module		
③ Tues ego ? appt with Head.		
④ Letter to field study centre.		

BS	1	2	L	3	4	AS
MON-DAY Dist. Dept. Meeting Agenda	2S ─ HN	h 6A	Joe Head appt. Friday PM ?	h 6B	3	Dept Meeting
TUES-DAY Assembly – Chairs!	4	Work on Tourism Materials		V6. Give out essay title	5 Chase Assesm. ·Sarah ·John H ·Sally.	PSE materials
WEDNES-DAY Collect data Resp. Qs	PSE	h 6A Data Resp Q. Tues Bid	James 12:30 office F/C	4 GCSE Assessment Marking.		Basketball Club
THURS-DAY	h 6B Data Resp Q field study letter.	4 Collect in textbooks	Tourism B'ball fixture. V. Grange 92167	3	2S. Collect Books / 2G HN	2S Books.
FRI-DAY	End Module Evaluation Sheets.	U6	Dept Meeting	Head – Tues Bid?	2G. Collect Books	
WEEK-END	2G Books Tourism Materials					

daily in-tray items which could have been disposed of at first handling (see R.A. Mackenzie, *The Time Trap*, McGraw Hill, 1975).

6   *Communicate*

Good communications are vital for effective management. Information and decisions must be passed quickly and efficiently to the people who need to know, both within your team and outside it.

How you choose to communicate information is up to you. Within your team you can use memos, a regular department bulletin, pin things up on a department notice-board, tell people personally, or use a mixture of approaches. The only test is: Do the people who need to know actually know all that they need to? Communications are so important that we deal with them in more depth in Chapter 6.

7   *Learn to say 'No'*

Some people find it very difficult to say 'No' to things. When they do, they feel guilty, even if the request is patently unreasonable. Yet if you take on too much you are unlikely to do anything effectively. It comes back to the key idea of determining your priorities.

In the Case Study on page 16 we saw how Chris Jones had got himself into the position of taking on too much. One of the reasons may well have been that Chris found it difficult to say 'No', both because he was not clear about his priorities and because he was worried about offending people by refusing requests. As a result he was under stress, and realised that he was neither being as effective as he should be, nor enjoying his work as much as he might be.

Here are four steps you can use when saying 'No'.

- *Listen.* Listen carefully to make sure that you understand the request, and to give the other person the courtesy of a proper hearing.
- *Say 'No'.* This means *really* saying 'No', not 'Maybe', or 'Perhaps', or 'I'm not sure', or 'I'll let you know tomorrow'.
- *Give your reason.* State your reason or reasons clearly so that the other person knows why you have decided not to say 'Yes' to the request.
- *Suggest alternatives.* If you can, suggest other ways the person might be able to tackle the task.

8 *Delegate*

Without successful delegation, successful management is impossible
(Gloucestershire LEA Advice to new Heads of Department)

In terms of how you organise and administer the work of your
department or team, you are making a rod for your own back if
you try and do everything yourself. The advice normally given to
managers is to delegate every task that you can (there will be
plenty left for you!). As a Head of Department you are responsible
for managing the workload of your department – that means
making sure that all the necessary tasks are done, not necessarily
doing them all yourself. If you delegate effectively you will have
more time to plan and do those jobs that only you can do.
Delegation is considered more fully in Chapter 9.

9 *Don't clutter up your spaces*
Do you recognise yourself in the following?

- *I know my desk is rather a mess, but I do know where everything
  is.* Possibly, but if you are taken ill can someone else find that
  vital bit of paper?
- *Oh yes, that memo you gave me last week . . . let me think, yes
  I'm sure it's in my pigeon hole somewhere . . . hang on a minute,
  let me just get all the rest of this junk out.* Why should someone
  else have to put up with this waste of time?

It is never easy to keep your work spaces clear, especially if you do
not have much space in the first place. But it *is* important to try –
your aim should be to have on your desk in front of you only what
you are currently working on. Not only does the cluttered desk or
pigeon hole waste time, it's usually also evidence of poor decision
making.

10 *An efficient filing system*
The sort of filing system you develop is up to you – it will depend
a lot on the facilities that are available to you in your school.
Whatever the system, unless it is efficient, you cannot hope to
discipline your decision making and streamline your administrative work. The importance of storage and retrieval are discussed in

more detail in Chapter 5 – Managing Resources. Two tests of an efficient filing system are:

- Can you find anything you need in seconds rather than minutes?
- Can you quickly explain to somebody else, over the phone, how to use the system to find something?

Case Study 4.2   *For action*
DEALING WITH YOUR PAPERWORK

This is what Simon Tucker, the Head of the Science Faculty, found in his pigeon hole on the first day of term.

- 3 Publisher's catalogues
- Invitation to a meeting at a local teachers' centre next week on *Science and Special Needs*
- Letter from a parent complaining that his daughter, who wants to be a doctor, is not being allowed to do three science subjects
- 4 Requests for option changes – to drop chemistry
- A promotional leaflet to heads of science/biology, from a company offering field trips in the UK
- Note from the school secretary to say that some books have arrived and are in the office
- Circular from the LEA publicising a newly-established link with the electronics department of the local polytechnic
- A curt note from Mrs Trevor, Head of Chemistry, saying that she must see you urgently
- Letter offering places for third years, on a first-come first-served basis, at local Young Scientist Conference – response by the end of the week

Simon has 30 minutes before the start of school to try and deal with this paperwork.

Use the 'Decision rules' (on page 39) to help you decide what Simon should do with all these bits of paper. (Remember: your aim is to handle each piece of paper only once if you can.)

Case Study 4.3   *For action*
ACTION PLANNING

When Simon Tucker arrived at school at the start of term he found the following tasks waiting for some action on his part, in addition to what was in his pigeon hole.

1 One lab is temporarily out of use because asbestos was found when minor repairs were carried out in the holidays. It will probably be three weeks before the lab is functional again. Most GCSE physics is taught in this lab.
2 The new textbooks for the fourth years have not arrived. There are also too few junior textbooks because many were not returned at the end of last term.
3 Mrs Trevor, the Head of Chemistry, is furious. She thought she had made it clear that she was not going to teach third year chemistry this year, yet she appears to be timetabled for it. She wants this error corrected immediately.
4 Miss Perkins says that she wants to see you as soon as possible. Apparently a sixth form tutor has unexpectedly obtained a secondment for the term, and Miss Perkins would like you to take over the tutor group.
5 There is a pleasant note on your desk from Mrs Gatlin, the Head, saying that £300 additional to capitation can be made available to the science faculty, but it would have to be spent by September 12 (five days time).
6 Rob Willis wants to see you urgently. He has had a letter from the hospital finally calling him for that operation on his ankle that he should have had during the holidays. He will be out of school from the end of the week for an indefinite period.

Put yourself in Simon's place. Decide how, and in what order, you would take action to deal with these tasks. Bear in mind the points that have been made in this chapter, and in particular keep in mind the key concepts of urgency and importance.

Case Study 4.4   *For action*
PLANNING YOUR DAY

Christopher Jones has just arrived at school. It is just after 8.15. This is what his programme for the day looks like.

8.40	Head's briefing for staff
8.50	Registration of form
9.00	Assembly
9.15–10.10	Period 1 – 6th Form A level
10.10–11.05	Period 2 – 3rd Year
11.05–11.20	Break
11.20–12.15	Free period
12.15–1.15	It has been arranged that Christopher takes the test to drive the minibus
1.15–1.25	Registration
1.25–2.20	Period 4 – 1st Year
2.20–3.15	Period 5 – 4th Year GCSE
3.15–3.30	Bus duty
3.30–5.00	Heads of Department Meeting
	Main item: *Should the structure of the school day be altered?*

In addition to the programme outlined above, Christopher has a number of jobs to deal with today.

- He had taken home his 4th year assignments to mark last night, so that they would be ready for Period 5 today; but his wife, Jane, had been most unwell and so he had looked after the children all evening, and had not even managed to start the marking. He is anxious to get it done before Period 5 if he can.

- The technician informs him that the apparatus he wants to use with his 1st Year group in Period 4 is not available. He will have to rethink the lesson.
- He supports changing the structure of the school day to 40 minute periods, and has prepared a working paper for the HoDs' meeting which outlines his ideas. This still needs to be duplicated and distributed.
- He had run a detention for Mabel Custard the previous evening, to deal with some 4th Year pupils who had been disobedient in class. Not all of them had turned up for the detention, and would need seeing.
- Simon Tucker, his Head of Faculty, has arranged a planning meeting tomorrow, to discuss how they should approach the issue of Balanced Science. Christopher had hoped to put some ideas down before the meeting.
- There are two messages in his pigeon hole.
  - *Please phone the Science Adviser today*
  - *Can I see you for a few moments today please?* (from the Head)
- Christopher really would like to phone his wife, who has a high temperature and was expecting the doctor sometime this morning.

Put yourself in Christopher's position.

1 *Bearing in mind the ideas we have looked at in this chapter, suggest how he should allocate his time during the day.*
2 *Devise a day planner to suit your own needs.*

Case Study 4.5   *For action*
CAN YOU SAY NO?

Simon is in his second term as Head of Science, and there are just under nine weeks to the end of term. He receives this note from the Head:

Dear Simon,

As you know I am very keen to improve the school's image in the local community, and as part of this whole approach I intend to change the way we have been holding our Open Day. Rather than having one day I want to hold some days/events at different times of the year, which are in effect open days.

I consider that it is particularly important to demonstrate the school's commitment to science, and so I would like to start the programme with a Science Fair at the end of this term. Naturally, as you are Head of Science I would like you to organise this event. I should also like to use this as an opportunity to extend our links with industry.

Could we please meet on Tuesday, Period 2, to discuss whether this is viable, and how we should organise it.

Brenda

Brenda Gatlin
Headteacher

How should Simon respond to this request?

Chapter 5
Managing Resources

As a middle manager you will not need telling that the management of resources is a major part of your job. The last decade has seen a significant increase in the complexity of this element of most middle managers' responsibility. In the broadest sense your resources could include people, time, money and materials – this chapter concentrates on the last two. These resources include textbooks, stationery, worksheets, exam papers, assessments, AV equipment, videos, software, and more. They all need to be produced, reproduced, stored, retrieved, evaluated, replaced – and most of all, available to the right people at the right time in the right place.

The management of resources is not made easier in many schools by the shortage of good storage space and facilities. As a middle manager, particularly if you are a Head of Department, you will need to think carefully about the systems you s t up to manage resources. In doing this, do not forget that *time* is probably the most important resource that you and your team need to use effectively.

In devising a system for the management of resources you will need to keep in mind four demands, which at times will certainly be conflicting:

1 The time you and your team have available
2 Convenience and ease of use
3 Cost effectiveness
4 Efficiency

The following situations illustrate how the four demands can come into conflict:

- The school's policy is not to allow pupils to take textbooks home. This may be the most efficient approach, but does it provide the best situation for teaching and learning?
- All team members are expected to file a copy of every worksheet they produce. In theory this sounds desirable, but is it a waste of teacher time in practice?
- The department makes substantial use of worksheets, rather than textbooks. This is cost-effective in the short term, but what are the implications, in terms of both cost and teacher time, in the longer term?
- All resources are kept in a central storage area. This may be the most efficient system in terms of stock control, but is it convenient and efficient for team members?

Storage and retrieval

Storage and retrieval must be considered together, as they are two sides of the same coin. It may be easy enough to find somewhere to store something, the trick is for anyone who needs to use it being able to find it quickly and without any fuss.

As a middle manager running a department or pastoral area you are likely to have varied storage and retrieval needs. There is unlikely to be a unified way of dealing with things as different as your administration papers, teaching and assessment resources of various kinds and pupils' work.

It is up to you to determine the most effective system to suit your needs, depending on what you have to store and what facilities you can make available. But remember, be ruthless – only store what you really need to.

What do you need to store?

In most schools storage space is at a premium. Anything that you make an effort to store must genuinely justify both the space it takes up and the time and trouble of storage and retrieval. Your first step might be to determine what you need to store, and what can be thrown away.

"Be ruthless, only store what you really need"

"If anything has dust on it, your suspicions should be aroused!"

If something has dust on it, then your suspicions should be aroused! Check with other members of the team, and then file it in the bin. In most schools it is remarkable how much storage space is taken up with resources that are never used. Don't fall into the 'It might come in handy one day' trap.

What kind of system do you need?

The storage system you use will depend on what you need to store and retrieve, and what facilities you can make available for the job. These are some questions you might want to consider when analysing your needs:

- *How often will this resource be used?* The more often it is used, the more accessible it should be.
- *Who needs to be able to use this resource?* The more people who need access to a resource, the more open its method of storage should be.
- *For how long will this resource need to be stored?* Combined with

the two points above, this should determine the type of storage facility a resource requires.
● *Who will be responsible for managing the storage of this resource?* Resources, especially if regularly used, need looking after.

The kinds of resources you need to store will vary, of course, but are likely to include the following:

Catalogues
Catalogues from publishers and equipment firms etc are often fairly bulky. When you receive a catalogue, glance through it rapidly. Then:

1 If there is nothing in it that is likely to interest you or your colleagues, throw it away.
2 If there is something that might be useful, take some action. Mark the page or entry in some way/order a copy of a book on inspection/circulate the catalogue to colleagues for comment/ information.
3 If it needs storing, file it and throw away the previous year's version. Keep all the catalogues in a box or series of folders, clearly labelled and in a place where colleagues have access to them. Have a purge once a year to remove all the outdated material.

Correspondence, minutes, lists etc
You need to devise a system that is flexible enough for all the different sorts of paperwork you have to store, and yet which enables you to store and retrieve information quickly. A filing cabinet is probably ideal, but a series of box files can be just as efficient. The key consideration is the *index system* you devise – the groups and sub-groups you sort items into. Two common groupings are:

1 By *topic* such as GCSE, divided into sub-groups such as coursework records/correspondence with exam group/moderation/results.
2 By *source* of material, using groups and sub-groups such as letters from parents/option choices/set changes/reports.

The important thing is that your system is clear and easy to use.

If some of your file headings could be ambiguous, make an index list which outlines where people could look for things. If necessary, put a cross reference in the file, marked 'See File heading . . .'. The acid test of your filing system is: Does it work – not just for you, but for everyone who needs to use it? *If you were unexpectedly off school and incommunicado for a month, could somebody else use your system without tearing their hair out?*

Teaching materials
Teaching materials may fall into two categories when it comes to storage: material that is regularly in use, and material that needs to be kept for future reference. Here are some of the points you need to consider when deciding how best to store such material:

1 Material that is regularly in use.
   • Can people get it without disturbing someone's lesson?
   • Can it be reached without shifting a lot of other things?
   • Does it have to take up prime storage space when not in use?
   • Should books or sheets be kept in strong boxes or folders for ease of transport around the school?
   • Do other users know where to find the material if it is not in its regular storage location? How?
2 Material for future reference.
   • If you want to keep worksheets, assessments etc for future reference, how many do you need?
   • If you use files/folders, do they discourage people from filing items? How often do you review the contents?

How open should your system be?

There are two problems here: how to keep track of resources, and the confidentiality issue.

With an open system documents or resource sheets may be removed and not returned. On the other hand, a system over which you have tighter control is more time consuming and indicates lack of confidence in your team members. The system you operate, and the rigidity with which you apply it, may well depend on the personnel in your team at any one time.

Confidentiality is a different matter. Some of the information you store – on pupils, reports on students and probationary teachers, references, appraisal documents etc – will be confidential. Only you should have access to this type of information. There is not usually a lot of this sort of information, but you will need somewhere to store it, such as a drawer, which you can keep locked.

On balance, however, the more open your system is the better. Not only are most school records becoming more open than in the past, but the members of your team are much more likely to work well with you if they do not think that you are keeping things from them, and if they know what is going on in the department. Another consideration is that, with an open system, you can delegate filing to other members of the department.

Keeping track of resources

Keeping track of all sorts of teaching resources is a problem for middle managers in most schools. To do it effectively can be very time-consuming, but not to do it can result in ineffective use of resources and high replacement costs.

There is no easy answer to the problem, and whatever system you devise must be tailored to your own particular needs. Case studies 5.2 and 5.3 focus on this issue.

Using computers in resource management

Computers provide obvious opportunities for information storage and retrieval. These opportunities will surely expand as more departments are able to buy their own computer hardware. However, using a computer may not necessarily save you time, at least not initially.

Before investing in a computer do seek specialist advice, as the best type of computer to buy will depend on what you want to use it for, who will be using it, and what other computer equipment is already in use in the school.

Some time spent on investigating how you could get the most effective use out of a computer is probably the best way to start if you are not already making use of this resource. It might be a useful exercise to persuade a staff member or advisory service colleague, who is interested in computers, to run a series of school-based INSET sessions on the ways departments could make use of computers. Some possible uses are outlined below.

Wordprocessing

This is almost certainly a useful area to explore if you have regular access to a computer at home or school. The sort of computers around in schools will certainly have wordprocessing programmes, although some are better than others. Using the wordprocessor to produce items such as standard letters, schemes of work, assessments and worksheets offers two significant advantages:

1 You always have a copy of the material on file, which can save you storing papers. (However, you may want to have a paper copy on file for easy access, and keep the computer copy as backup.)
2 You can make changes to materials quickly and efficiently, which will save you and others much time.

If you keep references or appraisals of other people on computer, the Data Protection Act (1987) requires that those people must have access to what you have written. You should notify your Head that you have such records on computer file.

Lists

A computer can be very useful for lists which need to be changed or updated frequently. There are easily operated spreadsheet programmes, for example, which will put pupils into rank order, or alphabetical order, or list them on the basis of form group etc. Again, you may need to seek specialist advice before making use of this sort of system, as what you get out is only going to be as good as what you put in.

A computer can certainly be useful if you want to keep a list of departmental resources which can be easily updated. As with normal filing you need to consider what sort of index you are going to need.

Design work

All wordprocessing software allows you to do at least basic design work, for example to produce worksheets with bold, italic and larger or smaller sized lettering. Computer companies are constantly developing new design software which will enable you to produce highly sophisticated material.

Case Study 5.1:   *For*
MANAGING YOUR RESOURCES   *reflection*

If you have not already done so, list all the resources available to your department. You may be surprised by the range and variety of the resources you possess.

The flow chart below poses some questions which may help you in the management of your resource base.

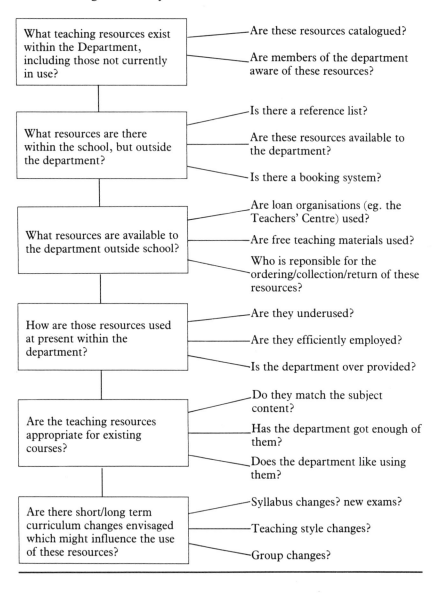

Case Study 5.2:   *For action*
A SHORTAGE OF TEXTBOOKS?

As Head of Department you have just received this letter from the parent of a 3rd Year pupil.

> I am sorry that Sally was not able to do her homework last night, but I am afraid she did not have a textbook to work from. I had in any case intended to take this matter up with the school. Sally says she quite often does not have a textbook for her work, particularly in your subject. Mr. Jones apparently tells them that they must share books. This is all very well, but it is not always possible, and I really do not think that Sally, or any other child for that matter, should have to try and do work at home without the proper books. I know that Sally gets very upset when she cannot do her homework properly, and I am sure other children do too. It makes nonsense of the system of homework.

As the Head of Department, how should you respond to this situation?

Use the problem-solving approach, outlined on page 14, to tackle this issue – someone else's ideas are outlined for comparison on the next page.

The sharing textbooks 'problem'

1 *Clarification*
   Problem: an apparent shortage of textbooks
   Symptoms: a) sharing of textbooks
                 b) homework not being done
                 c) parental concern
2 *Analysis*
   a) Is there a real shortage of textbooks?
      Is the teaching group larger than anticipated?
      Is the class teacher making the best use of available books?
      Have more books been ordered? If so, what is causing the delay?
      Is no departmental money available?
   b) Do all the pupils have to share a book?
      Is anyone else having trouble with homework?
   c) Have there been any other letters from parents?
      Is this also a problem in other teaching groups?

3 *Approaches*
   Possible courses of action include:
   • Buy more books (from local supplier for speed) or chase up books already ordered
   • Class teacher to make better use of existing books
   • Switch books from another group
   • Find alternative books as an interim measure
   • Affected pupils do homework at lunchtime till more books
   • Find a better sharing arrangement
   • Adjust numbers of pupils in teaching groups

4 *Action*
   Short term: Talk with class teacher – better organisation?
                   Reply to parent
                   HoD to chase up books/find alternatives
   Longer term: Review resource funding and provision in Year 3 in light of actual and projected pupil numbers

Case Study 5.3:
A SYSTEM FOR MONITORING TEXTBOOKS

Simon Tucker, Head of the Science Faculty at Bestwick Park, has just issued this memo.

SCIENCE FACULTY

MEMO   From: ST
                To: All members of the Science Faculty

ISSUING OF TEXTBOOKS
Can we try the following system?

1   Each department (ie Bio, Phys, Chem) will have their own ringbinder containing the textbook issue forms.

2   For each different title (if more than one textbook per class, as for example a Sixth Form) and for each class or set, complete one sheet (as attached).

3   We decided to include the column on the condition of books, although I am afraid it's more work for you. G = Good; F = Fair; P = Poor.
    If this proves too time consuming, we'll scrap it.
    On return of textbooks, you will initial if you think the condition then is reasonable.

4   Please explain to pupils that their signature indicates that they are prepared to look after the particular book they have received. They may NOT exchange it for anyone else's book, and they will return it in reasonable condition at the end of the year/course/module. Please also tell them, especially the examination year candidates, that the Head has agreed that pupils will have their exam results withheld if they have failed to return a textbook; and for those anticipating a return to next year's Sixth, the Science Faculty will not accept on its courses anyone who has not returned a textbook.

5   Would you also please check once a term (eg near the end) that each pupil still has the original textbook issued. Do not give any replacements without a 'big fuss', which will take the form of letters home, consulting with the Year Head, pulling out of toenails etc.

6   This will not overcome the problem of Easter leavers, non-examinees etc, but I will speak to Fifth and Sixth Year heads about ways to reduce these losses.

Bestwick Park High School Science Department: _____ **Dept**

Title: _____ **Teacher:** _____ **19**

Author: _____ **Class/Set:** _____

Pupil's Name	Tut. Gp.	Book No.	Date Issued	Cond'n G/F/P	Signature	Date Rt'd	Initial

1   *What is the issue Simon is trying to tackle here?*

2   *What are the advantages and disadvantages of Simon's system?*

3   *Comment on the way Simon seems to have tackled this whole matter.*

Case Study 5.4:   *For action*
A REDUCTION OF RESOURCES

Dear Simon,

As you know the authority is introducing its scheme to delegate more financial management to schools. In response to this, in conjunction with a committee of governors, I am currently undertaking a review of the school's use of non-teaching staff.

The committee have thought long and hard about the allocation of non-teaching staff, and one of their conclusions is that it will be necessary to make alternative use of one of the laboratory technicians hitherto allocated to Science.

The change will take effect from the start of next term.

Brenda

Brenda Gatlin
Headteacher

(NB The Association of Science Education recommends that one technician should essentially serve two science labs. On this basis until now Science has been somewhat generously resourced, but the proposed cut would leave the faculty slightly below the ASE recommended level.)

1   *How should Simon react to this letter?*

2   *Outline a management strategy which Simon could follow.*

Balancing the books

As a middle manager, particularly if you are a Head of Department, you will be responsible for spending some school funds. Your department will be allocated money from the school's capitation allowance, and it is your responsibility to spend this money in the most effective way to provide the best quality education. You will also need to account for the way money has been spent. There are three main elements involved in this task:

1   The process of determining the best way to spend the department's funds.
2   Keeping an account of the way money is spent, and balancing the books at the end of the year.

3   Evaluating your spending in relation to the department's needs
and priorities – so that you are in the best position to tackle (1)
again in the following year.

This whole process may seem somewhat daunting, but in fact it
need not be very time-consuming if you have your priorities and
systems sorted out. The task is becoming increasingly important
as Local Management of Schools (LMS) becomes a reality; LMS
gives schools far greater control over their budgets, which means
that there is a need for effective management at all levels within
the school.

Dividing the cake

Your first task is to determine the best way of spending your
funds. This needs to be done before any spending decisions are
made for your current financial year. Here are some points you
may need to consider:

1   How much money do you have available?
   • from capitation?
   • from any other sources?
   • are there any payments outstanding from last year?
2   What categories of spending do you have to cover?
   • photocopying/reprographics?
   • exercise books/file paper?
   • paper for school exams?
   • department visits/fieldcourses?
   • equipment replacement/audio-visual resources?
   • postage – for GCSE coursework/book returns etc?
3   What are your department priorities for spending?
   • how are you going to determine priorities?
   • who should be involved in determining priorities?
   • how will department priorities match school priorities?
   • how will money be allocated between 'priority' and 'basic'
     budget headings?

The way you decide how to divide your funds is up to you. A
good general rule is that, whenever possible, you should involve
all the members of your team in the discussion and determination
of priorities, and in the decisions about which actual resources to

buy. Case studies 5.6 and 5.7 focus on this issue.

At an early stage in your proceedings you might find it useful to allocate rough sums to all the budget headings you know you need to consider. Your evaluation of past spending will give you an indication of what you need to allow for 'basic' items. One departmental example is outlined in Figure 5a – this department had determined that GCSE textbooks had to be their priority in the coming year.

Capitation	£1300
less overspend from last year	120
	£1180
1 Stationery	<u>500</u>
exercise books	200
file paper	50
reprographics	150
equipment, AVA	80
postage	20
2 Textbooks	<u>600</u>
Sixth	100
GCSE	400
Third	–
Second	100
First	–
3 Reserve	80

Figure 5a

Asking for an extra slice of cake

There may be situations where you want to undertake a project or development which you feel is important for the department and school, but which you cannot afford to fund fully from your own money. In this circumstance you will need to make a bid to your Head.

If you are going to ask for more money you will be in competition with other people doing the same. You will have to justify your needs and argue for the bid you put in. To do this effectively you will need to outline your aims and objectives, and show how they relate to school priorities; outline your planned costings, and show how you are drawing on resources from a range of sources. An example of a bid is shown in Figure 5b.

Aim
To introduce a modular GCSE Humanities scheme, which will meet the needs of:
- the school's response to the National Curriculum
- the school TVEI proposals
- the Humanities Faculty development plan

Objectives
To undertake development work in the current year, including
1 INSET for the teachers involved
2 development of the syllabus, assessments & teaching resources
3 purchase of the necessary textbooks & equipment

Costings

		Funding source		
	Dept	School	TVEI	LEA
1 INSET				
8 days @ £75 supply cover		4 days	4 days	600
$(1+\frac{1}{2}+\frac{1}{2} \times 4$ staff)				
2 REPROGRAPHICS	100	100		200
3 OTHER RESOURCES	100	100	300	500
texts × 60 @ 4.25				(270)
texts × 40 @ 2.95				(118)
staff texts				(37)
equipment				(75)
TOTAL				
Consumables	200	200	300	700
Supply days		300	300	600

Figure 5b

Keeping the auditors happy

As a middle manager you will not normally be expected to keep immensely detailed financial records, but for your own benefit you need to keep track of your planned and actual spending during a financial year. If you run school visits or fieldcourses etc, which involve taking money from pupils or parents, you must keep a proper financial account of incomings and outgoings, so that at the end of the year you can produce a set of balanced accounts for the school auditors.

DATE ORDERED	DEL-IVERY	ITEM (TITLE/SUPPLIER/REF NUMBER/NUMBER/COST)	SCHOOL ORDER NO	ESTI-MATED COST	RUNNING TOTAL	ACTUAL COST	RUNNING TOTAL
16.6.89	✓	"PEOPLE IN THE INDUSTRIAL LANDSCAPE " KEMP + MACLEAN (MACDONALDS) x30 @ 4·95 ISBN less 15% discount	6034	126·00		126·25	
24.6.89	✓	OS MAPS (LONDON MAP CENTRE) 10 x 1:50000 AYLESBURY SHEET @ 2·25 10 x 1:25000 AYLESBURY SHEET @ 1·75	6061	22·50 17·50	166	24·00	160.25
24.6.89		FIELDWORK EQUIPMENT (GRIFFIN + GEORGE) 5x30m measuring tapes 0261612 @ 14·95 5 x clinometers 003472 @ 3·95	6062	73·25 19·75	259		

Figure 5c

Figure 5c is part of the accounts book of a school department. It includes these elements:

- the date when items have been ordered
- the school order number
- details of the items ordered: title, supplier's name/item cost/supplier reference number

- estimated order cost (remember to allow for educational discounts)
- record of delivery
- actual cost as invoiced (this may include price changes etc)
- running totals of estimated & actual expenditure

Keeping your expenditure under review

Towards the end of a financial year you need to review your expenditure during that year. We all know that we never have enough money to do what we really want or need to do! So it is worth spending some time with your team reviewing spending to see if there are any areas where you can save money, or switch money from one category to another. For example,

- Can you save on exercise books?
- Can you reduce expenditure on textbook replacements?
- What about the money you spend on photocopying?
- Can you share texts with another local school?

Carrying out a review will not only help you all to keep tabs on what you are spending, it will also put you in a better position to determine your priorities for the next year. As we keep saying in this book (and make no apologies for doing so!) the key to good management is to be clear about your aims, objectives and priorities.

Case Study 5.5:   *For*
ORDERING RESOURCES   *reflection*

There are a number of distinct stages you need to go through when you order new resources. The procedural flow chart outlines these stages.

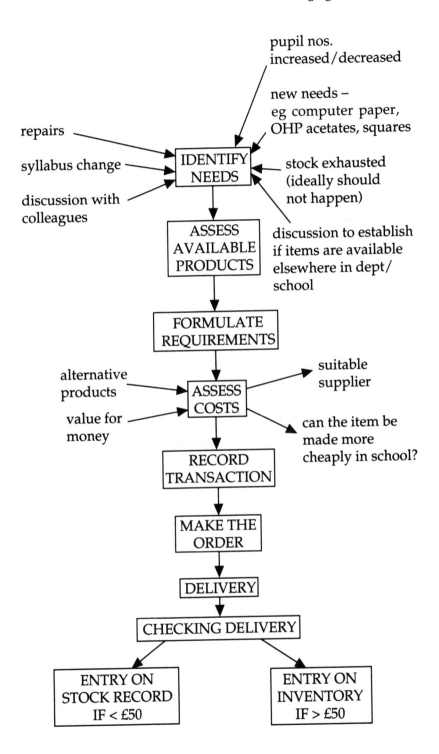

Case Study 5.6:   *For action*
ALLOCATING FACULTY CAPITATION – 1

MEMO

From: Yvonne Perkins – Deputy Head
To: Simon Tucker – Head of Science

Faculty and Department Capitation

I am now able to confirm that Science faculty capitation for next year will be £3 500.

I must remind you, however, that the faculty overspend last year was £240 (Physics £180, Biology £60), and that this sum will be deducted from this years capitation.

Your actual available capitation will thus be £3 260.

1   a) *What strategies are available to Simon for allocating the Science faculty capitation?*
    b) *What factors should he take into account in making an allocation between the departments in the faculty?*

2   *How should Simon deal with the overspend from last year?*

Case Study 5.7:
ALLOCATING FACULTY CAPITATION – 2

SCIENCE FACULTY MEMO

From: Simon Tucker
To: Heads of Chemistry and Biology

You will be pleased to hear that the faculty capitation for next year has been increased to £3 500. After taking into account our overspending last year (£240), we have an actual sum of £3 260 for next year.

Although I gather that it was the practice of my predecessor simply to divide the allowance equally between the three science departments, and leave it up to you how to spend the money, I would like to make different arrangements for this year.

I want to take the opportunity to review thoroughly the resources of the whole faculty, and so I have decided to retain central control of the money, and allocate sums to you for specific needs. This will also make it possible for me to allocate a substantial sum towards setting up the integrated science course in the first year.

In the meantime I would be grateful if each of you could let me have a list of the spending requirements in order of importance.

---

1   *Comment on:*
    a) *The possible motives for Simon's strategy.*
    b) *The tactics Simon has used to set up his scheme for allocating capitation.*
    c) *The possible advantages and disadvantages of greater faculty centralisation of spending.*

2   *What strategy should the Heads of Biology and Chemistry adopt? (Simon himself is Head of Physics).*

3   *If you were in Simon's place, what management approaches would you want to use to try and ensure that the scheme is introduced successfully and operates smoothly?*

Chapter 6
Communications

The importance of communications

In a large and complex organisation such as the typical secondary school, so much is happening all the time that good communications are vital. But unfortunately, as the following comments show, this is not always the case.

I always seem to be the last person to find out what's going on around the school – talk about poor communication. A first thought is that this teacher might be a bit of a moaner, who is taking a negative attitude. You might be tempted to respond 'Well, if he can't be bothered to make an effort to read things or find out what's happening then that's his tough luck' – after all, he can't expect to be kept informed without making any effort himself. But there is another side to this issue – communications are not something you can leave to chance or personal whim. **It is part of a manager's job to ensure that communication is effective.**

I don't think the Head has a clue what really goes on in my department, he's never asked me anyhow. There are two sides to this issue as well. Certainly a Head ought to know what is going on, at least in outline, and it is not good management if a Head of Department feels that the Head is not taking an interest in the department's work. This reflects poor communications on the Head's part. But why has the Head of Department not kept the Head informed and up-to-date about departmental work and developments? **Good communication has to be an active two-way process.**

I've just found out that the Science department has a unit on nuclear power, yet we do all that in Geography. The impression given by the speaker here is that the scientists should have known, or at least found out, that this topic was already being taught by the Geography department. Yet why should they know? Situations like this are common in school, and can be difficult to prevent, as there may be no formalised system of communication between the various departments and teams operating within the school. In such a situation it is part of a manager's job to **open and maintain informal contacts with people with whom an interchange of information could be essential.**

From these examples we can see that communications can take a variety of forms. They may be:

- *Formal* – where there is an established system for passing information, such as via a school bulletin, or regular meetings with a known composition
- *Informal* – the personal contacts one person has with others, often on an irregular basis
- *Upwards/Downwards* – information and ideas need to be communicated upwards and downwards through the school managerial hierarchy
- *Sideways* – it is essential that there are good communications between people in equivalent jobs, such as Heads of Year or Heads of Department
- *Oral* – in meetings, at interviews, in informal talks etc
- *Written* – in the form of memos, letters, reports etc.
  (The last two may have a very different impact, and often need to complement each other.)

To maintain effective communications, whether at department or school level, a balance between all these elements must be maintained. The two acid tests are these:

1 Can everybody find out all that they need to know at the least cost in terms of time and effort?

2   Does everybody feel part of a system of communication that is sensitive to their needs?

The following examples show some of the problems involved in getting the balance right.

- Theoretically you can keep people well informed by letting them know everything that they might conceivably need to know. However, in a school this might well mean that people are swamped with information, only some of which is relevant to their immediate needs. The result is usually that important bits of information are missed in the deluge.
- A Year Head needs to inform a tutor in her team about a new pupil, and does so orally when they happen to meet in a corridor between lessons. The information *is* communicated, but not in the right way. There is no harm in oral communication but in this instance the key need is for a written record of the information – a short note placed in the register or tutor's pigeon hole.
- A Head of Department needs to tell a member of his team that he has had to change her next year's timetable in a way that might not please her. He does so in a memo. The information *is* communicated, but not in the right way – in this instance the Head of Department owed his team member an explanation which really ought to have been done in a face to face conversation. There is nothing wrong in putting it in writing, but only after the courtesy of a personal explanation first.
- A Head of Department has received a letter from a parent about the homework set by one of the members of his team. He talks to the team member about it at the start of the next department meeting. He is probably right to choose spoken communication in the first instance, but has chosen quite the wrong occasion – it needed to be done at a private meeting, not in the formal setting of a department meeting with others present.

Your communications network

As a middle manager, whether a Head of Department, or Head of Year, or in some other post, you will have to operate an extensive communications network. The communications network of a Head of Department is shown in Figure 6a – it would be slightly different for other middle managers.

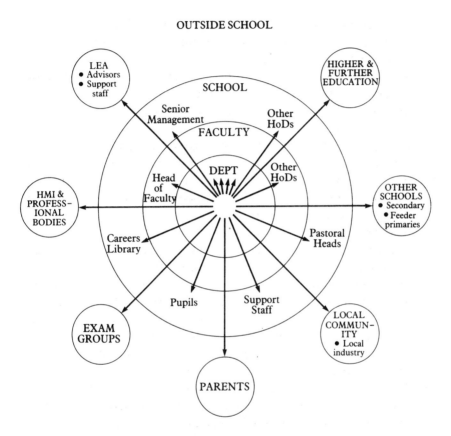

Figure 6a

As a Head of Department you do not have to communicate actively with all the groups all the time, but you should be aware that there will be times when you do need to. Generally speaking, the intensity and regularity of your communications will decrease away from the centre of the network. Communication with your team will need to be most intense, followed by communication with other people within the school.

Within your team

The system of communication you establish must be up to you, as it will depend on your situation and needs. A major means of communicating will be within the framework of team or departmental meetings; the management of meetings forms the basis of the next chapter in the book.

Within your team you will be communicating for a range of different purposes. The way you do it will depend to a large extent on the objectives you are trying to achieve. The four examples in Case study 6.1 give an indication of four main purposes of communication within the team:

1   To give information
2   To seek information
3   To discuss and exchange ideas
4   To build your team.

Case Study 6.1:   *For*
COMMUNICATING FOR DIFFERENT   *reflection*
PURPOSES

The four memos shown opposite were all sent between department or faculty colleagues.

1   *On the evidence of just these memos, which of the departments would you prefer to work in? Which department(s) might you prefer to avoid?*

2   *What is the purpose of each of these communications?*

3   *Comment on the style of each note, and on the extent to which each is likely to be effective in achieving its purpose.*

To:　All Third Year Tutors
From: Sunniti Pattni

Just a reminder about the team meeting after
school tomorrow - you will need to bring
your option choice folders with you please
for item 2 on the agenda.

Thanks

The Head says that we have got to talk
about multicultural education at the next
English meeting (again!).
At the HoD's meeting we were given this
paper from the advisory service - the
usual jargon and poor grammar as far as
I can see.

W. Bheasley.

Bill,
Where on earth is the folder on 'Lord of the Flies'?
I have been searching all over for it. I couldn't
find it in the English cupboard — nor could I
understand the intricacies of your filing system.
I know it was around at the end of last term.
Perhaps you could locate it for me. Priscilia.

Dear Martin
Just in case I don't have the chance to
see you personally — a quick note to say
thank you for all the work you put in for
the open evening. I thought the Humanities
area looked really good!
Well done! Vivienne

Case Study 6.2:
EFFECTIVE COMMUNICATION WITHIN THE TEAM

For reflection

From Sunniti Pattni, recently appointed Head of Third Year, to her tutor team:

Dear Colleague,

At our Year Meeting last week we all agreed that:

1 We wanted to keep our administrative tasks to a minimum
2 We do need a clear record of what is happening in the year group

I have been giving some thought to this since the meeting, and I have devised a 'weekly return' form to cover lateness, unexplained absences (no note) and uniform.

I have drafted it in longhand so that we can discuss it at our next meeting, and can amend it if we want to, before I get the office to duplicate a hundred or so forms for us to use.

I have tried to devise a system that will be easy to use! All you would need to do is to fill in the names and put the sheet in our Year pigeon hole each Monday morning. I shall keep a folder in my office filing cabinet (top drawer), clearly labelled and available to you, in which you can place your tutor group weekly return.

It would seem sensible for me to have a regular session with each of you to look together at the weekly returns – say once a fortnight. On this basis we could proceed to the next stage – letter home, detention etc as appropriate. This way we shall build up a clear and cumulative record, without involving any one person in a lot of paperwork.

If we agree on the system at our Monday meeting, I should like to see it set in operation at the start of the following week – the forms could be duplicated by then. Meanwhile I shall have had the opportunity to talk with Mr Brown (Deputy Head – Pastoral) and the E.W.O. about the scheme.

We could then run it through the rest of this term, and assess how it is working, and whether we need to make any changes or modifications.

Sunniti Pattni

The Head of Third Year's memo to her tutor team is an example of good practice. Her chosen means of communication – in writing – is the most appropriate, and further, the actual memo shows many of the characteristics of an effective communication:

- It outlines the issue clearly, and links the issue with objectives.
- The tutors to whom the memo is sent are treated as being members of a team – the writer uses 'we' much more than 'I'.
- Reference to a previous meeting shows team members that the writer has been listening to what people say.
- The style of the memo is open – the ideas are presented for discussion by all the team, so it is not a *fait accompli*.
- The style of the memo is positive – plenty of considered ideas are offered for the team to think about.
- Reference to practical details, such as duplicating and starting dates, gives people confidence that the writer has considered the administrative implications
- The writer indicates that she has also communicated with key people outside the team – the Deputy Head and Educational Welfare Officer.

Is your department visible?

'Visibility' in this instance is used in the advertising context – how is the work of your department or area viewed by people from outside your team? People who work in marketing and advertising work on the principle that, no matter how good a product or service, it is worthless if potential consumers do not know about it, or if they have a false idea of it. It is all a question of *image*. The situation in school is not quite the same, of course, but the concept of visibility is important.

What we are talking about here is a form of public relations – not the over-the-top 'blowing of one's own trumpet' form of PR, but a sensible realisation that you have to work to let people know what you stand for and what you are doing.

As a Head of Department or Year Head, your own reputation and the reputation of your department or area will be closely linked. What impression do you and your department give to others? For example, how would you rate other people's impressions of your department in the following aspects of school work and life?

well-organised . . . . often inefficient
welcoming of new ideas . . . . .resistant to change
effective with all   not very good with certain
  sorts of pupils . . . .   types of pupils
forward looking . . . . complacent
friendly and welcoming . . . . insular and unwelcoming
plenty of initiative . . . . .only following others' lead
thoughtful and sensitive   often insensitive and
  to other people . . . .   thoughtless
much involved in   semi-detached from much
  school activities . . . .   that goes on
only concerned with   concerned for the good of
  the department . . . .   the school as a whole

How do you think the following people or groups would view your department? Would you have made any impression at all, one way or another, on some groups?

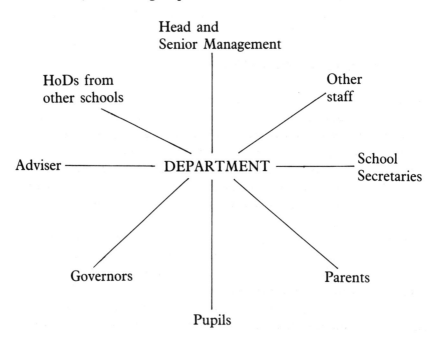

To be mindful of PR and your visibility does not mean that you are trying to create a false image. Other people are going to form an impression on you and your department whether you want them to or not. Their impression will be based on what they see and hear. What we are arguing is that you need to be aware of this and to work to shape the image other people have of you. We do not suggest that you should be doing this as a personal or departmental ego trip, but because a department or team with a negative image is less likely to be effective in providing a high quality educational service – and that is the ultimate aim of all of us in education. What impression do you and your department give?

- *Do people outside your team hear you? If so, what is it that they hear?* For example, do you come over to others as someone who is more often positive than you are negative – are you a 'can do' person? As a middle manager, you clearly have to look after your departmental or team interests, but do you come over to others as someone who is only interested in your department, perhaps even, at times, appearing to obstruct things that would be good for the school overall?
- *When people see anything that comes from you or your department, what impression does it give them of your work and standards?* For example, what do your department documents look like? Do you actually have the up-to-date department documents that you should? When you send people memos or notes, what do they look like – are they written on a scruffy bit of rough paper, or do you have proper departmental memo slips?

When it comes to visibility it is up to you to make a positive effort. You cannot afford to leave it to chance. You certainly need to keep the Head informed, not only about what you and your department are currently doing, but also about your ideas and plans for future developments.

Department documents

The current changes and developments in education place much emphasis on accountability and the availability of information. A range of people, including parents, governors and the Secretary of

State, have the right to know about the work of your department. Do you have the documentation available to meet these needs? Can you answer 'Yes' to the following questions:

- If an HMI arrived in school tomorrow and wanted information about your department, would it be available to her?
- If a new pupil joined the school from abroad, what document would your department have to explain your syllabuses to the pupil and his parents?
- If the Head decided to study the file of departmental documents that should be in her filing cabinet, would yours be there and up-to-date?

What kinds of documents are you likely to need?

1   *A department document*
This document is aimed primarily at the members of your team. It should set out:

- departmental aims and objectives, linked to school aims and objectives;
- the roles of the members of the department;
- how the department operates and administrative procedures;
- department resources and their locations.

2   *A syllabus*
The syllabus may cover all parts of your work, or separate syllabus documents may cover phases such as Years 1–3, GCSE, Sixth Form, etc. The syllabus is more than a statement of course content – some ideas for the headings that should be included in a syllabus are outlined in Case Study 6.3 on page 80.

In addition to the syllabus, the members of the department who teach particular years or parts of a course, will need a *scheme of work* which provides more detail than the overall syllabus can give.

3   *A document for parents*
This should be a short, concise document, free of jargon, so that parents can understand the department's philosophy, organisation, approach and syllabus. It needs to include information about

how the teaching groups are organised, how pupils will be assessed, and what pupils will be studying.

4 *A document for other staff*
This document is for senior staff or pastoral staff who will need to explain and outline your subject to pupils, for example, when it comes to option choices. This document will also provide a reference for colleagues from other curriculum areas if they want to find out what your department teaches.

5 *Entries in school brochures*
You will be expected to write and update your department's entries in the school's various booklets and brochures.

There is no one right approach to writing each of these documents, although you will need to follow the school's house style. These are some points you might bear in mind:

- *Audience.* Who is the document aimed at? This will influence your use of language and technical detail, and the design and style you adopt.
- *Design.* What impression will it give to others? What is the most effective design and medium of production? Will the finished document look attractive and accessible?
- *Drafting.* How will you make the document clear and concise? Plan it out first, so that you know what you want to say.
  Keep it short.
  Avoid jargon wherever possible, and try and express complicated ideas as simply as you can.
  Divide it up into sections, and head each section clearly so that the reader can follow the organisation of the document.
  Summarise points at the end (or at the end of each section), this makes a long and complex paper easier to understand.
  When you can, use diagrams or flow charts to help express complex ideas.
  Ask someone else to read it through at the draft stage, to check for mistakes, and whether you actually say what you think you say!
  Finally, check again that you really have included everything that you need to say.

Case Study 6.3:   *For*
THE DEPARTMENT SYLLABUS   *reflection*

This is the list of section headings which a group of Heads of Humanities Departments agreed should be included in a department syllabus document.

Aims
What are the main aims of the course?
How do these aims relate to the general aims of the school?

Objectives
How is the department/faculty going to achieve these aims in terms of:

- identifying *key ideas*
- defining essential areas of *knowledge and understanding*
- identifying key *skills* to be developed
- recognising important *values and attitudes* (both of the pupils themselves and of the people who contribute to the issue under study) which should be raised

Methods
The syllabus should identify the range of teaching and learning strategies which will be used to achieve the syllabus objectives. Appropriate methods should be linked to particular objectives.

Structure
Details of how the course is to be subdivided (for example, into modules or themes) and about the timing of course segments.

Differentiation
A statement about how pupils of differing abilities will be enabled to show positively what they know, understand and can do; this should include clear criteria for the assessment of success at differing levels.

Assessment and record keeping
Details of the assessment and profiling procedures, both during and at the end of segments of the course, and how the outcomes of

these assessment procedures are to be recorded and shared with pupils and parents.

Evaluation
A statement of the procedure that will be used to review the success of the course in terms of such criteria as:

- meeting aims and objectives
- timing and coverage
- organisation
- resources
- interest and enjoyment
- contribution to whole school aims (including such issues as equal opportunities and special needs)

Progression
A statement about the relationship between the course and work pupils will have done previously (including work done in feeder primary schools), and also work that is to follow. It is important to show that progression is planned and not just accidental.

Cross-curricular links
Details of how the course relates to the total educational experience of the pupils, including the cross referencing of concepts, skills and values to other areas of the curriculum.

Resources
Details about the resources available for the course, including written resources, visual resources, computer software and the resources which can be drawn from the local area and community.

Case Study 6.4:
A DEPARTMENT DOCUMENT

For
reflection

Bestwick Park School: Biology Department Document

The Biology Department has three general goals for our pupils

1   To provide a worthwhile educational experience for all, whether or not they are intending to study Biology at a higher level.
2   To provide a suitable preparation for careers which require a knowledge of Biology.
3   To provide a suitable foundation for further studies in Biology and related Sciences.

Specific aims

1   To develop an understanding of essential Biological principles based on knowledge of living organisms and their environments.
2   To encourage a respect for all living organisms and their environments.
3   To stimulate an attitude of curiosity and scientific enquiry.
4   To develop an appreciation of Scientific approaches and methods including:
    a) Making and recording accurate observations
    b) designing, carrying out and assessing simple practical investigations.
5   To develop an awareness of the effect of human activities on these relationships.
6   To develop an ability to use these skills to identify and solve problems related to Biology.
7   To appreciate the relationship with applications of Mathematics, Physics and Chemistry to Biology.
8   To develop an interest in and an enjoyment of the study of living organisms.

Organisation of teaching

The First and Second years participate in the General Science programme. Pupils are taught in their form groups, which are mixed ability. Learning support is provided in the classroom by the Learning Support Department.

Third year pupils receive two Biology lessons a week. Teaching groups are based on broad ability bands and the lower band groups are significantly smaller than upper ability bands.

A Science column in the option choices scheme ensures that all pupils study Science until the age of 16. Fourth and Fifth Year GCSE groups are roughly banded where there is more than one group operating at the same time.

Allocation of teaching groups is rotated among the department.

Examination courses
In the Fourth and Fifth years pupils take either CO-ORDINATED (BALANCED) SCIENCE leading to TWO awards at GCSE or INTEGRATED SCIENCE leading to ONE GCSE award (Southern Board). A substantial element of Biology is included in both these courses. The courses are designed to encourage a wide variety of scientific skills and the Biology section will include fieldwork.

The department has a long tradition of offering A Level (London Board) and this course always attracts a good take up.

Teaching strategy
The Biology department believes:

1 Biology is an exciting subject
2 The pupil's own motivation is the secret of successful learning.

We aim to provide a positive learning environment. Pupils are encouraged to develop a questioning approach through the medium of practical exercises and problem solving. Extensive use is made of all kinds of source materials and audio visual aids.

Assessment
1 It is department policy to set one marked homework per week. Other homework will of course also be set, but every pupil will have a minimum of one piece of work marked by the teacher weekly.
2 In accordance with school policy end of year/course examinations are set. It is our policy to set a common paper for each year group.
3 GCSE pupils receive a formal assessment test at the end of each topic in accordance with course requirements. Third year pupils will also be tested in this way at least once in each half term in order to prepare for GCSE.
4 No profiling projects as such have as yet been introduced into the department, but we hope to be able to introduce a profiling scheme in the near future.

Discipline
As a department we support the view outlined in the staff handbook that the basis of good discipline lies in good teaching – an appropriate curriculum, good preparation, well structured lessons etc. and in plenty of positive reinforcement. Should a discipline problem occur in a Biology lesson, the Head of Department is always the first point of reference.

1 *Consider the effectiveness of the document in terms of content and style.*

2 *What changes would you want to make to the document?*

Case Study 6.5:   *Exemplar*
INTERNAL COMMUNICATION – A DEPARTMENT BULLETIN

One way of saving time at department meetings and a good way of conveying information on minor matters is to produce a short but fairly frequent department bulletin. This is particularly useful for large departments or faculties. It does not remove the need for personal contact or meetings, but is a good way of dealing with administrative trivia or notices that can fill a lot of time at a meeting. It does not have to be a great work of art, but could easily be produced on the department banda machine. It is a job you do not have to do yourself, but could allocate to a junior member of the department, but you must make sure that the person who is responsible for producing the bulletin has access to all the necessary information.

Bestwick Park High School:
The Social Sciences Faculty. Bulletin No. 3 Nov. 19—

1 *Mock exams*
I now have most of the outstanding papers in for mock exams, but GCSE Sociology and A Level History are still outstanding. Please see that these reach me without delay or let me know what the problem is.
   I am hoping to have all the duplicated papers back by the end of the week. C.D.

2 *Class visits this month:*
First Year visits to the British Museum.

I AB – Wed 15th Mr Blake & Mrs Michael.
I PM – Thurs 16th Mr Parks & Miss Prince.

3 *Members of the Faculty out on courses*
Wed 22nd. Clive Draper is attending Computers & the Geography Department, at the local teachers' centre.

4 *AVA*
The cassettes ordered for the beginning of term have finally arrived.

5 *Viewing session*
The History Department have arranged to view their new videos on Monday lunchtime, 12.30–1 p.m. They may be of interest to others in the faculty. Date: December 13th, December 20th and December 27th. Each video lasts approximately 20 minutes.

6 *Dates for your diary*
Faculty meeting: Nov 28th. Room 113. Time 3.30. Agenda and working papers to be circulated according to normal procedures.

7 *A message from Vivienne Michael*
I am delighted to be back with you after my long absence. Thank you very much for all your presents and the greetings, especially the lovely flowers you sent me when the baby was born. I shall be holding an informal get together for the Faculty on Tues 14th at 12.30 in Room 113. Wine and light refreshments provided. I hope to see you all there. Please let me know if you can't make it.

Case Study 6.6: *Exemplar*
AN ORGANISATIONAL CHART

The organisational chart illustrated overleaf shows the structure, and main individual responsibilities, of the Science Department at Bestwick Park School.

This is a simple and effective way of communicating the organisational structure of a large department, faculty or pastoral team. It provides the sort of information that might need to be communicated to colleagues within the school (and indeed to newcomers within the department), and also on occasion to parents and outside bodies.

BESTWICK PARK HIGH SCHOOL • THE SCIENCE DEPARTMENT

Organisational chart

SIMON TUCKER – HEAD OF FACULTY
HEAD OF PHYSICS

CHRISTOPHER JONES – HEAD OF BIOLOGY
special faculty responsibility
= profiling/pupil assessment

Nigel North – Biology
special faculty responsibility
= Information Technology

Mabel Custard – Biology
special faculty responsibility
= Greenhouse project

LABORATORY TECHNICIAN
Doreen Massey

HELEN TREVOR – HEAD OF CHEMISTRY
special faculty responsibility
= exams co-ordinator

Robert Willis – Physics/Chem
special faculty responsibility
= Junior science

George Lamb – Physics/Chem
special faculty responsibility
= AVA stationery

LABORATORY TECHNICIAN
Sandra Hughes

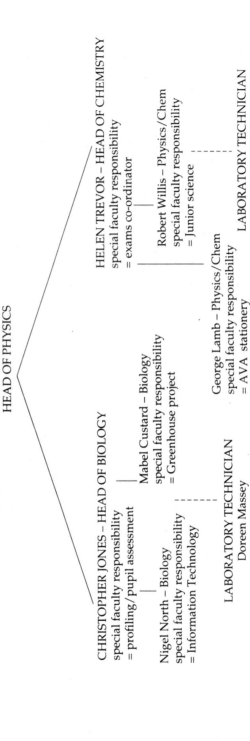

Chapter 7
Meetings, Bloody Meetings

Case Study 7.1:

AN UNSUCCESSFUL MEETING

*For
reflection*

From a conversation between Frances Marshall (Second in the Modern Languages Faculty) and a friend about the faculty meeting held earlier that day . . . .

'I knew when I saw the agenda that we were in for a long session – 12 or 13 items, and some of them looked as if they might take a lot of time and discussion, though there was no indication which were meant to be the major items. I was worried about this because, as you know, I had to get back to school again by 7.00 pm because Gwen and I were taking a party of sixth formers to the German play at the university. There weren't any pre-meeting papers either, which would have helped me to understand or make my mind up about some of the items, but I didn't anticipate that the meeting would be quite as bad as it turned out to be.

When I got there Roger had already arrived and spread his papers all over the teacher's table, and the others had taken up seats in the front row of the pupils' desks, so I joined them, but I felt uncomfortable. Keith didn't do it like that – we all sat round a table together – it was much easier for planning, and much friendlier. I hadn't had time to grab a cup of coffee on the way to the meeting, and had hoped that

Roger would offer us some refreshments. Keith always used to provide coffee and biscuits, which made a nice start, and kept us going if it turned out to be a long meeting. I made a mental note to suggest to Roger that he should revive that custom.

Thinking about food had distracted my attention for a bit. When I started to listen again we were on 'Matters arising from the last meeting', but we seemed to be going back over everything we had discussed last time. I suggested that this was wasting a lot of time as we had already made decisions about these items, and that we did have a lot of other business to get through; but Roger gave me a lecture about it being important to get things right and not skimping discussion. I think he thought that I was trying to stampede him, so I shut up.

The meeting meandered on. Gwen spent ages discussing problems that had arisen from the GCSE orals, which was not on the agenda at all, and when I pointed this out Roger snubbed me again. I think I had expected Roger to be a more effective chairman. He simply did not seem able to move the meeting along at all. I began to speculate if there was a course for chairmen that trained you to be able to allow everyone to offer their opinion without going on for ever, and actually to reach decisions as well. By this time I was despairing of the meeting ever ending, as well as feeling hungry and extremely irritable, and I began to feel that sending Roger on such a course, preferably immediately, would be money well spent!

This led me to wonder whether Roger was sensitive about his authority as HoD, and whether he felt threatened by me in some way. In spite of what he had said about listening to everyone's views, he seemed to be belittling everyone's suggestions in the same way that he had put me down, yet he didn't seem to have much to offer himself. This had an inevitable effect on Gwen, who, as you know, can be difficult at the best of times, and we were subjected to a lengthy diatribe on how she felt that the division of capitation between the three languages in the faculty was unfair, and that now we also had to bid for INSET funds, she supposed that French would continue to favour itself at the expense of German and Spanish. Fernando seized on this on behalf of the Spanish department and there was a real row between Gwen, Fernando and Roger. It all seemed to me totally unnecessary as a simple formula based on the number of pupils taught by each subdepartment could easily serve as a basis for discussing the allocation, and we could set this against changes in syllabuses etc, or other external factors, which might affect our INSET needs. After the way Roger had snubbed me earlier, however, I didn't feel prepared to intervene again, and in the end the matter was just left as nobody could agree. That meant that the INSET bid didn't get settled at all, which is a nuisance as Mrs Gatlin is quite likely to deal with department bids on a first come, first served basis.

We had another row about who should receive training first in using the new department computer, and another long and rather acrimonious discussion about our methods of teaching and learning. This got nowhere, and then at around 5.30 we had to sort out our attitude to prizes. This took another half an hour, and I had to abandon all hopes to going home before the play. Yet I noticed when we were discussing prizes that if Roger had simply put the issue to a vote at one point fairly early on in the discussion, he would have got agreement; but he just let the discussion continue endlessly, and, as far as I could see, aimlessly. I could not understand what he thought he was doing. Discussion is all very well, but we needed to make some decisions. We did not even reach 'Multicultural Education' which was No 11 on the agenda, and I am sure that this was the item that Mrs Gatlin meant us to spend most of our time addressing. The whole meeting seemed to me to be total waste of time and energy. It did nothing to improve faculty relations, and it didn't settle any of the things that we were meant to sort out . . .'

Frances did not enjoy that meeting, and considered it a total waste of time. It is not difficult to see why it was not a successful meeting, as Roger made a series of classic mistakes:

1 *The day*
Was it really a good idea to have the meeting on a day when Frances and Gwen were giving up their evening to take out a group of pupils? This kind of thing is one of a number of

indicators that Roger's treatment of his colleagues was less than sensitive. That day may well have been the one designated on the school calendar, but a responsive Head of Department could have made arrangements to change it (remembering of course to notify the Head).

2   Timing

Roger was prepared to let the meeting run on until 6.00 or later, which is quite unreasonable. He seems not to have heard of the guillotine, nor of directed time (1265 hours).

3   Agenda

The agenda was too long, and was not structured. Most school meetings last between 1–1½ hours. How did he expect to get through all the items in one meeeting? In the event they neither finished, nor reached an important item which was put on the agenda at No. 11. The agenda had not been prioritised, and items had not been given time allocations.

4   Papers

No papers had been drawn up and distributed before the meeting, so nobody had the chance to think through items beforehand. In the meeting every agenda item had to be fully explained, which wasted valuable time.

5   Arrangements

Roger did not create a positive atmosphere in the meeting. Some refreshments at the start would have helped. His seating plan automatically created a 'me and them' situation, and so it is hardly surprising that confrontations developed.

6   Chairing

Roger chaired the meeting ineffectively and ineffectually.

- His timing was poor – 'the meeting meandered on'. Each item took a long time to discuss and the agenda was not finished.
- He was not always in control of the meeting; 'Matters arising' turned into a replay of the last meeting (an ominous sign!). Items were raised and discussed which were not even on the agenda. People interrupted and argued with each other.
- His approach was negative – he seemed to put down everyone's

suggestions, which resulted in friction between himself and the various individuals present. He gave no encouragement to people who might have had things to offer.

- The fact that Roger himself seemed to be able to offer little in the way of ideas meant that the meeting had no chance of gaining a sense of purpose and direction.

7 *Decision making*

The discussions did not result in decisions being taken. Everyone put forward their views, but no consensus was reached; nor did Roger seem able to grasp where a solution could have been reached by taking a vote. Thus the meeteing did not achieve anything, and the people there went away feeling frustrated and disillusioned.

In short, Roger Russell's faculty meeting was badly prepared and badly chaired – an object lesson in how not to run a meeting!

Managing meetings – some pointers

You cannot just list a whole lot of things to talk about on a bit of paper, call that an agenda, summon people together – and then expect the meeting to be a success. Before you arrange any meeting, you need to ask – and answer – a number of questions.

- *Why* are you holding the meeting? What are your objectives?
- *Who* needs to be at the meeting?
- *What* should be on the agenda? What materials do people need to have?
- *When* is the best time to hold the meeting?
- *Where* is the best place to hold the meeting?
- *How* does the meeting need to be conducted to create the conditions most likely to achieve its objectives?

These questions form the basis for the following ten 'pointers' to things you should consider.

1 *Always prepare thoroughly for a meeting*

A great deal of planning and thinking needs to be done before a meeting takes place. This is particulary true of meetings at which important or complex changes, or potentially complex issues, are going to be discussed. Our most important piece of advice is **always prepare thoroughly for a meeting**.

2   *Keep the objectives of the meeting clearly in mind*
A meeting should be held for a purpose. Department and team meetings are usually held with the following objectives:

- to deal with administrative matters. This kind of meeting will convey information/give instructions/deal with organisational planning/agree procedures
- to provide a forum in which important issues are discussed. This kind of meeting could be used to seed new ideas/analyse and evaluate existing practice/identify and try to solve problems/decide policy questions
- act as workshop. In this kind of meeting the department will engage in a group activity, such as the planning and production of course assignment and assessment materials. You may be able to timetable some workshop time using your school-based INSET allocation.

In reality, life may not be as neat as this. A meeting called for one purpose may need to include some other elements. A meeting not intended to concentrate on administrative matters may often have to deal with urgent items before it can move on to the real business of the session. In such cases, the important thing is not to get sidetracked and spend too long on the minor issues. An agenda which indicates a time limit for each item will help here.

If you are planning a major change you are unlikely to be able to realise your objectives in just one meeting. You will need to arrange a series of linked meetings around the theme, and take this into account in your planning. But remember, **always keep the main objectives of the meeting clearly in mind**. Further, we must stress that meetings are held for different purposes, and **different types of meetings need different approaches**.

3   *Get the number of meetings right – not too many, not too few*
An overlong agenda could mean that the team is having too few meetings. However, there is no right answer to the question 'How often should department/team meetings be held?'

As a manager of other people's work you must provide regular opportunities for your team to be consulted and informed about developments. Some departments have an informal chat over coffee or lunch once or twice a week. 'Break with cake' is a feature of one successful Science department that we know. This kind of short, informal session is a useful way of dealing with much of the day-to-day business of the department; it also keeps team members in touch and helps to build the team.

Longer, more formal meetings will need to be held to deal with major issues – the frequency is up to you. If you are lucky you may have a team meeting timetabled as part of the school day, but it is more likely that your school will have calendar slots for after school meetings in directed time – often one every half term. Quite possibly you will not find this sufficient and will need to arrange at least one more session per half term.

Whatever pattern of meetings you settle on, **make sure that you are not holding too many.** Review you pattern of regular meetings from time to time. What would be the effect of not holding this meeting? Is there an alternative means of conveying this sort of information?

4 *Organise your agenda so that it helps you*
The agenda is your programme for the meeting, your scheme of how the meeting is to be structured. If an agenda is to do this job effectively, and so help you run the meeting, it must be more than just a list of items. Some key elements for an agenda include:

- the date, time and place of the meeting
- a list of the people who should attend – indicating if anyone is to take a major role in the meeting
- a note of what kind of meeting it is to be – information, administration, policy making etc
- a note drawing people's attention to accompanying documents which should be read or brought to the meeting
- a list of the items to be discussed, with some indication of importance, and possibly timing
- provision of an opportunity for items to be suggested as additions to the agenda (eg 'Any other business')
- where appropriate, an indication of how the previous meeting was followed up

There are various ways of setting out an agenda (some examples are considered in Case study 7.2 below). Having drawn up a suitable agenda, make sure that it is published or distributed long enough before the meeting, to allow people time to think about the items so that they can come prepared. It is also a good idea to send a copy of the agenda to the Head, so that she or he is kept informed of the department's work.

5 *Make sure that everyone can come*

It is counterproductive to hold a meeting from which several of your team are absent for whatever reason. Having a regular meeting slot, and informing people of occasional meeting dates well in advance, can help to overcome this problem. You should expect people in your team to let you know well in advance if they are unable to attend.

If someone is absent, make sure that you or a colleague is named as the person who will brief that person on the main points of the meeting. If you give the impression that it is just hard luck for the person who is absent, then you will be giving the wrong messages about the importance of what is discussed at your meeting – ie that it does not really matter that much that someone was not there.

Do not forget any part-time colleagues in the team. Try and fix your meeting cycle so that part-timers can be involved as much as possible.

6 *Organise the room and resources*

How the room is arranged can influence the meeting by determining, for example, its formality or style of discussion. Think carefully about the style that is going to suit your needs best.

- *The circle of chairs* is often a good arrangement for a discussion session or a fairly informal meeting. Everyone can see each other's faces which helps to build up group identity.
- *Sitting around a table* is slightly more formal than the circle of chairs and some people favour this as being more business-like. This arrangement is best when you are going to go through a working document or when people are going to have to write as well as talk. It is not suitable when a larger number of people will be attending.
- *The classroom arrangement* is the most formal. It is usually only

effective when there is a larger number of people at a meeting whose main purpose is as a briefing session. It is easier for the chairperson to direct the meeting, but discussion is inhibited by people sitting in rows.

Make sure that all the papers you need to give out are ready to hand. Similarly if you are going to use a visual aid, make sure all is set up beforehand. Being disorganised yourself gives powerful messages of quite the wrong sort!

7   Anticipate possible difficulties

Give enough thought to what you want to get out of the meeting – what are the end-products you are looking for? Anticipating possible difficulties is part of your preparation work.

- Do you have all the information you may need in order to discuss particular items on the agenda?
- Have you thought about the possible arguments and counter-arguments people might put up? The way you, or others, present a case and back it up in discussion, could be crucial.
- If there is an agenda item that you know could be controversial, it is worth sounding out people's opinions beforehand – you are not trying to stifle discussion, but to prepare yourself so that you can make sure people's views are given a fair hearing.
- On important policy issues it can be useful if you give some thought to how far you are willing or able to compromise if the going gets tough.

8   Develop an appropriate style for chairing meetings

There may well be a mismatch between your preferred style of chairing, and that to which your team is accustomed; or between what you normally do and what is best suited to a particular type of meeting. Some ideas on the skills of chairing are outlined in more detail later in this chapter.

In chairing a meeting you are trying to blend the two roles of referee and leader, which is not always an easy task. The important thing is to be flexible, so that the style you select is the one most likely to achieve your objectives for the meeting. Remember that different types of meetings require different approaches.

For example, you may wish to give your team members experience in chairing and reporting meetings. This would mean that you rotate the chair and the person taking the minutes from meeting to meeting.

However, if there is a particularly sensitive issue to be discussed you may wish to take the chair yourself; this would be a perfectly sensible decision, but be sensitive in the way you handle the change in routine.

9 *Record the main points of discussion and the decisions taken*

Keeping some form of minutes or record of all but the most informal meetings is important. This record is needed beause:

- it avoids disagreement or confusion over what was said and the decisions that were taken
- it lists the actions agreed on, and who should take them
- it can be used as a means of informing people who were not present of the main points of discussion and decision
- it can be used as a checklist for progress reports at the next meeting

It is up to you to decide how the minutes are best set out, and who should take them – it can be a good idea to rotate this task among your team to give everyone experience of doing the job.

The main thing about minutes is that they should be clear and, above all, concise. At the same time they should genuinely reflect the major contributions different people made to the meeting.

10 *Evaluate the meeting*

The only way to develop your skills of organising and chairing meetings is to analyse and evaluate your performance. You can do this for yourself by using a checklist of questions such as:

- What were my objectives for the meeting?
- Were those objectives achieved?
- If not, what went wrong?
- At what point did things go wrong?
- What could I have done to prevent difficulties?
- What have I learned from this meeting which will influence the way I organise meetings in future?

You will also want to gain some feedback from your team, as their ideas on how a meeting went will not always match yours! It is also worth organising for someone external to your team (another Head of Department colleague, perhaps) to come and watch, but not participate in, one of your team meetings. This colleague can act as a process reviewer, and analyse the meeting with you afterwards. Alternatively, you could arrange for the meeting to be videoed. This gives you an invaluable opportunity to spend some time analysing the interaction between you and your team, and betwen the team members themselves. If you do go for some form of external evaluation exercise, you must let your team members know beforehand that the appraisal is aimed at you, and not them.

Six skills for chairing effective meetings

1 *Be businesslike*
- Have everything to hand that you are likely to need.
- Keep your eye firmly on the time – move the meeting on where necessary.
- Make sure that decisions are reached – do not let the meeting dwindle into a talking shop.

2 *Communicate clearly and persuasively*
- Explain ideas clearly – don't get bogged down in too much detail, or you and everyone else will lose track (a supporting document is the place for details).
- Be persuasive – but don't be too overtly partisan, as you need to be seen to have a balanced view.
- Know your arguments, and have the information you need to back up what you say.

3 *Listen carefully to what people have to say*
- Meetings are to allow discussion – don't let it become a monologue, from you or anybody else.
- Make sure that everyone has their say and show that you value each contribution – make eye contact with the speaker and show that you are listening carefully.
- If one person tries to dominate the discussion, or be dismissive of others' views, intervene firmly but politely.

- Be positive by inviting and rewarding contributions – you can reward the effort of contributing even if you want to remain neutral on the views expressed.
- Don't be negative – resist the temptation to score off other people, and don't start with a mind closed to others' ideas.

4   *Focus the discussions*
- Clarify and reinforce objectives.
- Summarise progress.
- Build on good ideas.
- Work for agreement and consensus.
- Structure decision making.

5   *Think on your feet*
- Be flexible enough to react immediately and positively to good ideas, or to offer a counter argument for consideration.
- Be sensitive to the mood of the meeting – when to be firm, when to be relaxed, when to use humour.
- Think about your body language – what messages are you giving?

6   *Keep cool, calm and collected at all times*
- Don't lose your temper with people who are being difficult – yet be firm and determined.
- Defuse tension before it develops too far – the meeting is about policy and issues, not individuals.
- Be tactful with people who are angry or upset – keep your cool at all times, as nothing will be gained by responding in kind.

Case Study 7.2:   *Exemplar*
DIFFERENT AGENDA TO SUIT DIFFERENT MEETINGS

Example A

Bestwick Park School
GEOGRAPHY DEPARTMENT

Agenda for Department Meeting, Feb 4
3.30 pm, Geography Room

1 Apologies for absence

2 Minutes of the last meeting

3 Matters arising

4 Report back from HoD's meeting (CD)

5 Introducing mixed ability teaching into the Geography Dept (main item)

6 A.O.B.

This is a traditional agenda of the kind often used in school and other meetings. It is not very informative as it consists mainly of routine items. The major topic appears as Item 5, and it is highlighted; however, there is no indication whether this is merely for discussion or if decisions need to be taken at the meeting. There is no indication of whether any form of discussion paper has been circulated and needs to be brought to the meeting. There is a danger with this form of agenda of the discussion getting bogged down in earlier items, such as 3 and 4, leaving insufficient time for the main discussion item.

Example B

Bestwick Park School
LEARNING SUPPORT DEPARTMENT MONTHLY MEETING

Place: Learning Support Centre (R55)
Time: 3.30 pm
Date: Wednesday Feb 3

1 Left overs from the last meeting

2 Tracy's report on the progress of the building work for the centre

3 Petronella's reports: (a) Introducing the home learning scheme
                         (b) Progress on learning support library

4 Frank's report on the new worksheets

5 Individual pupils – progress & problems

This agenda is less formal than the first example. It dispenses with minutes and other formalities, though it does build in some time looking back at the last meeting. No one item appears to be more important than the others. There is a clear indication of who will be responsible for the various sections of the meeeting. The overall objective of the meeting is limited – it is mainly a briefing/report back session on the various current areas of the department's work.

Example C

Bestwick Park School
SOCIAL SCIENCE FACULTY MEETING

Date: March 9   Location: Library
Time: 3.30 pm – Guillotine at 5.00 pm
To: All members of the Social Science Faculty

Timing	Item	Method	Who	Resources	Action
10 min	Arrangement for faculty field trips	Check list to prevent clashes & OK arrangements	Clive	List circulated	Implement
20 min	Recent AV acquisitions	Review at meeting	Roger		Viewing session
60 min	Moving to a multicultural curriculum	Discussion	Vivienne	Paper circulated	Follow up in separate dept meetings

---

This is a highly structured agenda, in which the objectives, timing and organisation of the meeting are made clear to everyone. The primary purpose of the meeting is to discuss a major development in the faculty curriculum, and ample time has been allowed for this in the arrangements. Participants have been given a preparatory paper to read before the meeting, and are reminded to bring it with them so that it can form the basis of discussions.

Example D

Bestwick Park School
SCIENCE FACULTY MEETING

To: Simon, Helen, Nigel, Mabel, Rob, George, Christopher

November 4, 3.30–5.00 pm, Science Prep Room B

Chair: Helen
Secretary: Rob

Priority		Who	Item	Time guide
1	A	Helen	Mock exam papers	10 mins
2	A	Simon	Introducing profiling	30
3	A	Chris	Integrated junior science – progress review	20
4	A	Nigel	Uses of the new computer	15 demo
5	B	George	Stationery needs	5
6	B	Helen	New expense forms	5
7	B	Nigel	The case for a wordprocessor	10
8	C	Rob	The new General Science film	20 view if time
9	C	Helen	Discipline in the Lower School	15
10	C	Simon	Course available Nov–Dec	5
11	C	Mabel	Greenhouse project report	5

At this meeting the role of chair and secretary rotate. Clearly the agenda has been compiled after giving everyone the chance to contribute items. There looks to be rather too much on the agenda – but to deal with this the items have been listed in priority order (A = essential, B = important, C = can be left till next meeting). The timing looks tight on some items, but it is indicated as a guide only. One weakness of this style is that it is not always clear about the precise purpose of each agenda item.

Case Study 7.3:   *Exemplar*
MEETING MINUTES

Bestwick Park School
SCIENCE FACULTY

MINUTES
November 23 Meeting

Present: Simon, Helen (Chair), Christopher, Nigel, Rob (Minutes), Mabel
Apologies: None

1 MOCK EXAMINATIONS
The timetable for having papers typed and reproduced was gone through, and it was decided who should be responsible for papers/parts of papers, and how marking should be organised.
ACTION: list to be circulated by HELEN

2 PROFILING – LOWER SCHOOL
Simon showed us a number of different kinds of profile, which were discussed. No one was fully happy with any of them as they stood, and it was decided that we should try and design our own.
ACTION: CHRISTOPHER & NIGEL to work on a draft profile for the first meeting of next term

3 INTEGRATED JUNIOR SCIENCE
Christopher went through a list of possible topics for the first year of the course, and these were discussed. Helen was not sure that this arrangement would stretch the bright pupils sufficiently, and some amendments were made to the original list – this was then agreed.
ACTION: SIMON & ROB to produce a topic each for the December meeting, MABEL to assist Simon

4 DEMONSTRATION OF THE NEW COMPUTER
Nigel demonstrated some of the things the new computer could do. It was generally agreed that this was very useful, but that most people needed more time to get to grips with this. Nigel agreed to try and spend some time with us individually on this.
ACTION: ALL – see NIGEL to fix a time for this when convenient

5 STATIONERY

The stationery order, produced by George, was checked and approved.

ACTION: GEORGE to put in order

6 EXPENSES FORMS

Helen explained how the new forms have to be filled in.

ACTION: ALL – use them!

7 WORDPROCESSOR

Nigel put forward a case for the faculty having a wordprocessor, stressing its administrative and creative values. We all agreed, but Simon pointed out that there was no money left this year.

ACTION: no action possible now – review in April

8 A.O.B.

All other business carried over to next meeting. Simon will circulate courses list. Meeting closed at 5.05 pm.

This example of a set of minutes illustrates how the agenda shown in Case study 7.2 – Example D might have worked out in practice. Some points to note:

- The minutes are used to record the follow up strategies agreed at the meeting. The minutes record both who is responsible for the next stage, and the time scale involved.
- The Head of Faculty, Simon, is not trying to do all the follow up work himself – it is being divided among the faculty members. The probationer is being involved by being asked to work with the Head of Faculty.
- The people who agreed to prepare a draft profile are given half a term for the task, as it is a substantial job. Small jobs, on the other hand, are given much shorter, or immediate, time scales.
- Despite the delegation involved Simon must retain some important oversight functions. At some time before the next meeting he will need to check how much of the agreed 'action' has been done – there may be people who are in difficulty with the deadlines.
- Simon has delegated the production and distribution of the minutes to Rob, but it does remain Simon's responsibility to ensure that the minutes get distributed without undue delay –

within a week to 10 days after the meeting. In certain instances Simon may want to glance over the minutes before they are printed.

Chapter 8
What Style of Manager Are You?

What people say about . . .

Mr Smith – the Head
He is certainly very efficient – all the paperwork gets done, and things are organised to the last detail. He's not so good with people – maybe he's a bit shy, but he seems awkward and sometimes rather tactless when he talks to staff. I think he would much rather send round another memo than actually talk to us.

Mrs Jones – the Deputy
What a lovely person! Her office door is always open to anyone, and she's always prepared to help you out with a problem – she really is the most unselfish person. There are a few times when the exams and the substitution gets into a bit of a muddle, but with her workload that's hardly surprising.

Miss Carter – Director of Studies
Some people find her rather formidable, but she certainly knows her job. She's always prepared to listen to requests, and you always feel that you have had a proper hearing. When she has decided she always explains her reasons. Firm but fair is her approach.

Mr Brown – Head of Middle School
The kids are frightened of him, and if truth be told, so are some

of the staff! If you are one of his tutors, and he thinks you have done something wrong, he will certainly tell you about it. He has his system, and he sticks to it – I suppose it works well enough, but it doesn't make for happy tutors.

Getting the balance right

The thumb-nail character sketches above are all of people we have worked with over the years. In their own ways they were all at least reasonably effective in their jobs, some more than others. Each of them had a very different style of management.

This chapter looks at some of the elements that make up management style. We are not necessarily saying that one style, or one characteristic, is better than all the others, as what works in one situation may not work in another. The most important thing is for you to be *aware* of your own particular style of management, and about the effects it may have on the people you work with. Only with such self-awareness can you be in a position to try to modify your management style to increase your effectiveness in the particular situation in which you are working.

The authoritarian/laissez faire axis

AUTHORITARIAN _____ DEMOCRATIC _____ LAISSEZ
FAIRE

One of the key elements of management style revolves around your behaviour towards the people who work in your department or team. At one end of the axis you have the *authoritarian* (the 'Napoleon'), while at the other end you have the *laissez faire* manager (the 'Anything goes' person). Occupying the middle ground you have the democratic manager.

Some of the typical characteristics of management styles along this axis are outlined in Figure 8a.

> **Authoritarian** managers are:
> High on + telling
>   + instructing
> Low on - consulting
>   - accepting
>   - delegating
>   - team building
>
> **Laissez faire** managers are:
> High on + leaving people to do
>   their own things
> Low on - setting objectives
>   - controlling
>   - delegating effectively
>   - team building

Figure 8a

Figure 8b describes the range of leadership behaviour.

The MacGregor axis

This axis is so called because the idea was first outlined by an American management consultant, Douglas MacGregor (*The Human Side of Management*, McGraw Hill, 1960). It is a useful complement to the behaviour axis outlined above. The MacGregor axis is based on the notion of your assumptions about people's likely behaviour, which in turn is a key factor in the level of motivation you are likely to produce in the people in your team. MacGregor divides managers into two main categories:

MacGregor 'X' ←——————→ MacGregor 'Y'

The MacGregor X Manager Assumes	*The MacGregor Y Manager Assumes*
• People naturally don't want to work	• People are innately motivated
• People are not interested in improving their performance	• People naturally want to do well

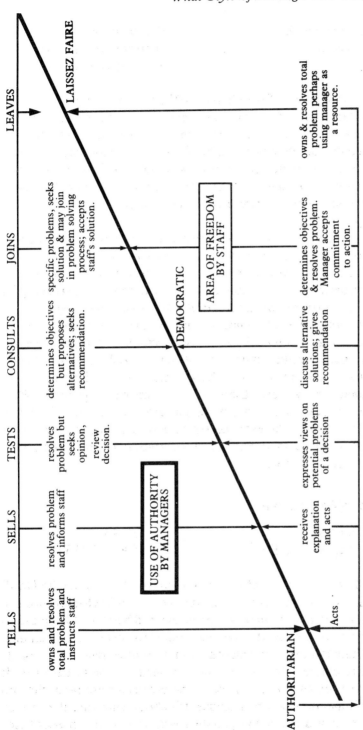

Figure 8b Continuum of Leadership Behaviour

- People need close
  supervision

- People are always
  interested in improving
  their performance

We all know that if people take a MacGregor X view of us, this has a depressing effect on our motivation and self-esteem. A MacGregor Y view of us may well improve our motivation – provided the conditions are right for us to develop and perform.

Authoritarian managers tend to be MacGregor X (*'People won't understand it, you know . . . I can't trust people to do what I ask them . . . It won't work as there are always some people who won't do it properly'*).

Laissez faire managers are usually, but not always, MacGregor Y (*'I just let them get on with it, they can do it just as well as I can . . . The job gets done doesn't it? . . . I leave that to so-and-so, so have a word with him'*). They can be MacGregor X, however (*'It's not worth bothering about, as nobody does what I ask anyhow . . . There's no one with any spark so I just let them get on with it'*).

What are the implications of the MacGregor concept? We are arguing that a middle manager with an outlook tending towards MacGregor Y is much more likely to motivate and involve a team of people. However, there is an important proviso. Real motivation only comes when people are clear about what they should be doing – the extreme MacGregor Y laissez faire manager can be just as demotivating and frustrating to work with as a MacGregor X authoritarian.

The people-task axis

PEOPLE   TASK
ORIENTATED ←――――――――→ ORIENTATED

If you look back to the character sketches of Mr Smith (the Head) and Mrs Jones (the Deputy) at the start of this chapter, we can note that their *work priorities* are clearly different. The Head is strongly task-orientated – his main concern seems to be planning and administration; the Deputy, on the other hand, is strongly people-orientated – her main concern seems to be to help people whenever she can. Both of these characteristics are laudable, but not in isolation. Good management is about achieving the task by using the resources of the people around you – this means being effective in managing people and managing the task. Figure 8c shows how some of the other management characteristics we have been considering can be linked to the people-task idea.

Figure 8c

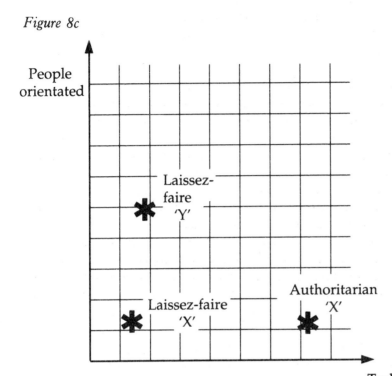

The **Authoritarian X Manager** is likely to be strong on task (s/he has a clear idea about what needs to be done) but weak on people (people are told what to do, and expected to follow set procedures).

The **Laissez Faire Y Manager** is likely to be weak on task (people are left to get on with their own things) but fair on people (on the whole people are quite happy with the arrangement as they are trusted to do the necessary).

The **Laissez Fair X Manager** is weak on both task and people (there is no clear direction or leadership, yet people are not allowed to get on with things on their own, with the result that they are frustrated and unhappy).

None of the three stereotypes outlined fall within the most important sector of the diagram – the upper right sector, which shows that the person is strong on both task management and people management. Neil Miller has christened the people who fall in this sector the *Omega managers*.

The Omega Manager concept

Figure 8d shows how Miller divides managers into four broad categories. Three types we have come across already – the *authoritarian*, the *do nothing*, and the *country club* managers. ('Country club' is the name Miller uses for those managers who run happy teams, but teams which underachieve in terms of the tasks they have to perform.)

The fourth category Miller terms the *Omega* managers (Omega, the last letter of the ancient Greek alphabet, means 'all things'). The Omega manager is not all things to all people, but he or she does manage to combine effective management of both the task and the people. We will be looking in more depth at some of the ways this can be done in the chapters on *Managing people* and *Team building*.

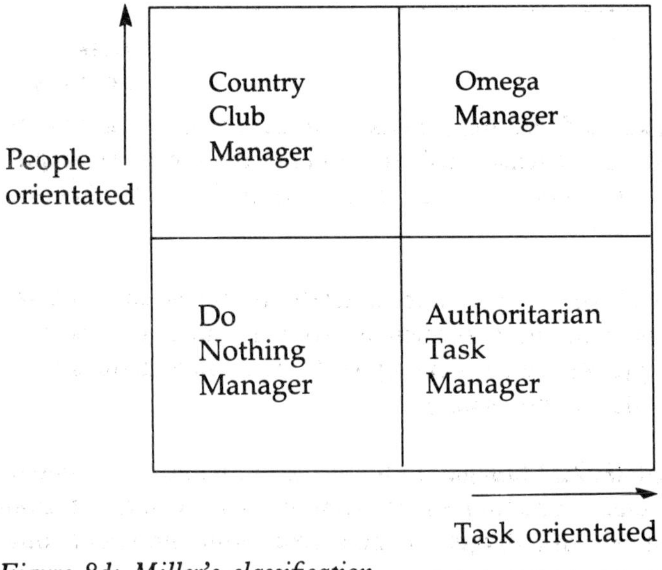

	People orientated	
	Country Club Manager	Omega Manager
	Do Nothing Manager	Authoritarian Task Manager

Task orientated

Figure 8d: Miller's classification

The two extremes . . . the authoritarian and country club managers.

What characterises the Omega manager? These are some of the things the people who work with Omega managers say about their department, and about their team leader:

About the department
We have really high standards in the department.

I feel that I'm really making a contribution to the department.

We know what we are trying to do.

It's good to have clear objectives, it helps you to concentrate on the most important things.

Department meetings are always open, everyone is listened to.

It's good to be able to rely on other people – in the department things usually get done on time.

We don't always agree on things, but when we don't we have a good argument to thrash out policy.

It gives you so much more confidence when things are going well.

We always set targets for what we plan to do, and then we spend some time evaluating our efforts.

About the team leader
She really does listen to what we have to say.

He works hard, and expects the same from us.

She is good about thanking you for what you do – it's always nice to feel appreciated for things you really have done well.

If she feels that you are not doing something as well as you should, then she will say so – she's firm but fair.

He's not afraid to make difficult decisions.

There's no doubt who is the leader of the team, but we are all made to feel that we are contributing.

In summary

There is always a danger when one analyses management styles that one will stand accused of oversimplification. There may be something in that criticism, but we would argue that it does not invalidate the exercise. What we have aimed to do is to start you thinking about different management styles, and about the possible impact of such styles on the people with whom you work.

A common criticism is that analysis of management styles does not take into account that the same person displays different behaviour in differing circumstances. Quite so, a manager will, and indeed ought to, adapt his or her style to differing situations or in relations with different people. What we are suggesting is that the first step must be for you, as a middle manager, to be aware of the way you operate in a range of situations. A second step can then be for you to consider whether you should be modifying your behaviour in order to make your management style more effective. No doubt some Omega managers are born Omega – but on the other hand plenty of Omega managers become Omega by a process of self analysis, and by learning from their mistakes.

Look back at the four character sketches outlined at the start of this chapter. We hope you would agree that, simple and brief as they are, the characters ring true – they ought to as they are based on people we have worked with! Analyse the management style of each character, on the basis of the ideas outlined in this chapter.

Authoritarian . . . . . Democratic . . . . . Laissez faire
MacGregor X . . . . MacGregor Y
Task-orientated . . . . People-orientated

Into which of Miller's four categories would you place each person?

Case Study 8.1: *For action*
TWO EXAMPLES OF MANAGEMENT STYLES IN ACTION

'But nobody took the chair . . .'
(From a conversation between Vivienne Michael and Meriel Hemmings)

'I was shadowing Bob Wade (Deputy Head, with responsibility for Staff and Curriculum Development), as part of my own training for senior management posts. He took me to a curriculum development meeting he had convened on Technology.

The meeting was about introducing a modular general course as part of the Fourth Year curriculum. It was the group's first meeting. There were four Heads of Department present, and Kate King, who is the school's Technology Manager. The meeting started as soon as we arrived, but what I found so surprising was that nobody seemed to be in the chair. Each person took it in turns to say what they had planned as the scheme of lessons for their own module. Then they began to explore how they might build links, and a scheme for a cross-curricular initiative involving the four departments began to be tentatively formed.

I kept expecting Bob or Kate King to intervene and give direction to the project, but they didn't. The Heads of Department sometimes asked Bob a question about class sizes or resources; Kate or Bob occasionally asked for a statement or idea to be clarified if it looked as if some people were perplexed, but apart from that they just listened.

Kate seemed to be taking notes, and towards the end Bob suggested that she should produce a record of the meeting. The group then discussed what would be appropriate for that record; it was agreed that they didn't want minutes as such, but that Kate should produce a summary of what had happened at the meeting, and the decisions taken, so that this could be available at the next meeting. Kate also offered to produce a critical path analysis so that each person could see how their module would fit into the overall scheme, and to expose problems of timing or linkage. This idea was welcomed and adopted. It all seemed to happen so fast, yet there appeared to be no-one directing operations. I've never seen a meeting work like that before.'

'He treats us like children . . .'
(From a discussion among form tutors)

'We have to go to Mr Brown's office once a week after school. He sits behind his desk to chair the meeting, while we sit facing him in hardbacked chairs, just as if we were pupils in his class. He gives us our orders for the week. It is a briefing session, and we are given the minimum of information to do the job, clear instructions about precisely how and when he wants things done, but no explanation whatsoever about why we are doing most of the things. He is a very good organiser, but we never discuss any of the issues, and he takes all of the decisions himself without consulting us.'

Analyse the two accounts.

1 *What management styles are in operation?*
2 *How effective are they in the circumstances in which they are employed?*

Case Study 8.2:
LEADERSHIP QUALITY

A group of teachers and advisers were asked to suggest ways in which to monitor the effectiveness of the management and leadership qualities of middle managers in schools.
Their ideas are outlined in the document below.

Monitoring effectiveness – quality of leadership

Elements
In any assessment of leadership quality, in whatever educational situation, the group suggested that there are three key elements. These elements are distinctive but not discrete.

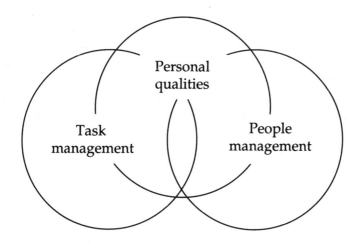

Indicators
The group's aim was to identify, during a school review exercise, possible positive indicators which would point towards an effective leadership by a middle manager.
The group considered that it could be counter-productive to generate too many indicators, and has aimed to suggest about six for each element of leadership quality.

People management

1 *Strong team identity.* Is there a clear sense among people of belonging to a team?
2 *Clear communications up and down.* Are information and ideas properly communicated among all team members?
3 *Shared aims and objectives* within the team. Are all team members clearly aware of team tasks/aims/objectives?
4 *Open discussion within the team.* Can team members voice differences of opinion without disturbing the effectiveness of the team?
5 *Individual expertise is valued.* Are the particular skills/expertise/ qualities of team members recognised and used? Are weaknesses minimised?
6 *High morale.* Is there a positive attitude among all team members in relation to the team tasks?
7 *Team visibility.* Does the team have a clear and recognised identity amongst people who are not in the team itself?

Task management

1 *Aims and objectives.* Are the team aims and objectives clearly defined in writing? Are these aims and objectives derived from school aims?
2 *Decision making.* Is the process of decision making in the team effective? Is there evidence that decision making involves all team members?
3 *Review and evaluation.* Are there clearly defined processes whereby the team's work and aims/objectives are reviewed and evaluated?
4 *Task achievement.* Is there evidence that previously defined team tasks have been taken through to a successful conclusion?
5 *Deployment of resources.* Is there evidence that the team's resources (time, space, money) are effectively deployed? Are resources fairly deployed within the team?
6 *Strategic planning.* Is there a means by which the team undertakes long-term planning?
7 *Team meetings.* Is there a pattern of properly organised meetings, formal or informal as appropriate, with agenda and minutes where necessary?

Personal qualities

These would be some of the personal qualities and expertise shown by an effective middle manager.

1 Positive attitude
2 Self-confidence
3 Sensitivity to others
4 Ability to delegate
5 Broad educational perspective
6 Classroom competence
7 Curriculum/pastoral expertise

On the basis of what you have read in this chapter, comment on the document the group produced.

Chapter 9
Managing People

I found the sixth form A level work so stimulating that I barely noticed that I was working two lessons more than my allocation should be. I've waited years for the chance to teach A level. Previously, under Bill's regime, all the sixth form work used to be divided up between him and Vera.

(English teacher)

I should never have insisted that Helen took that second year group when she was so set against it. She has taken every opportunity to tell me when it isn't working, and why not.

(Head of Science)

Mr Brown only ever tells us what to do, he never asks for our ideas or what we think. I don't feel involved at all.

(Member of year team)

What I like is the way that my Head of Department is always ready to discuss a problem with me. He doesn't talk down to me, it's more a sharing of ideas. I've learnt a lot in a short time and I'm really enjoying being in the Biology department.

(Biology teacher)

The trouble is that Margaret talks at us, not to us. She never listens to what we say, she is always so busy telling us her latest scheme.

(Second year tutor)

It is not difficult to draw some general, yet very important points from the quotations above.

- People like to be consulted about what they have to do – on the whole they do not like just being told what to do.
- People who are motivated are going to be more positive about their work, and are likely to be more effective in what they do.
- One of the most important qualities of an effective manager is the ability, and willingness, to listen to what people have to say.
- If people are enjoying their work, and feel that what they are achieving is worthwhile, they are likely to be more tolerant of less than perfect working conditions (and few schools can claim perfection!)
- Deciding when to use your authority as a Year or Department Head requires sensitivity – heavy-handed use of authority is often counterproductive.

No doubt you could add more. How you work with, and manage, the people in your team, is perhaps the most crucial element in your role as a middle manager.

In the education system it is the human resources which consume the most investment.
(Everard and Morris, 1985)

It is largely up to you to create and maintain the conditions and atmosphere in which people are motivated and work with a sense of purpose. In this chapter we consider some general points about managing and working with people; in the next chapter we focus more specifically on the building of effective teams.

Ten pointers on how to manage people

1 *Spend time getting to know the people for whom you have a management responsibility*
Invest plenty of time in getting to know the members of your department or section. Your knowledge of, and concern for, the people in your department will not only help you to run things

effectively, but will also bring you loyalty from the members of your team.

Take the time to find out about people's professional skills and experience. Find out something too about their home circumstances, and their interests – but do this sensitively, without prying. This knowledge will help you to know what you can legitimately expect of them, and gives you an indication of where they might need help and support. A few well-chosen, sensitive words to show someone that you are aware of difficulties, either at school or at home, can make it so much easier to deal with a difficult member of the department. Showing that you are interested in them, as people and as professionals, will encourage the members of your team to offer you the support that you will need to do your job effectively.

2   *Communicate, and explain things clearly*

Do not have professional secrets. It is important that your department members do not feel that they are being kept in the dark about what is happening. In earlier chapters we have stressed that regular and open communication is an essential part of your task as a manager. Talk to your team about any plans or schemes, and ask for their ideas, before you talk to your senior managers or the subject adviser. You are less likely to win people's support if they feel left out of the process.

Always explain things clearly. People are much more likely to co-operate if they know what they are supposed to be doing, and precisely what is expected of them. Always explain, in whatever way you think best, exactly what your plan or idea is, how it should work, what the time scale is, what results you anticipate, and the part each person has to play in the overall achievement of those results.

3   *Allow plenty of opportunities for exchange of views*

It is usually helpful not only to brief your team thoroughly, but also to allow them the chance to talk things through in a free and open exchange of views. This is psychologically important, and can be a real safety valve to allow people to air their worries and concerns. When there is no dialogue people may begin to mutter behind your back, and this can lead to disaffection within the team.

4 *Be prepared to take decisions*

Although it is important to discuss things within the team, as a middle manager you must be prepared to take decisions. A lot of these decisions will be about fairly minor matters. Whenever you can, deal with these immediately and then make sure that everyone in your team knows what the decision is, has a chance to comment if necessary, and is clear how it affects them.

Some decisions will require rather more time and thought, but they too will need resolution. Taking sufficient time to make a good decision is one thing – being indecisive is quite another. Being indecisive is fatal if you want to be an effective manager of people. How democratically you take decisions has to be up to you, and depends on the nature of the issue and/or the state of development in your team. We would argue strongly, however, that the more people are involved in the decision making process the more likely they are to support what you finally decide should be done.

Once made, decisions do not necessarily have to be as immutable as the laws of the Medes and the Persians. If you find that you really have got it wrong, the best policy is to change things as fast and efficiently as you can; but do try not to do this too often!

5 *Cultivate a calm and positive image – stay cool!*

Do not make mountains out of molehills. If you treat most problems as local difficulties which you expect to be able to solve, two things are likely to follow: first, you are more likely to be able to find a solution quickly and efficiently; second, you are more likely to win the respect and support of your team members. Few things are more annoying than to have someone pretend that a minor difficulty is a major problem, and for that person then to demonstrate their brilliance by finding a solution to this 'major' problem for you!

Always try and keep your cool. Train yourself not to flap or lose your temper if you want to be a successful manager of people. Keeping a clear view of the problem and of your objectives is so much easier in a calm and positive atmosphere – the problem-solving approach we have suggested could help you here. Few things will contribute more to a loss of your credibility as a manager than too many outward signs of panic!

6   *Lead by example*

You cannot expect other people to do what you are not prepared to do yourself. If you are allocating extra work or responsibilities to your team you must be seen to be taking on extra work yourself – if you do not, then you can only expect grumbles and a reluctance to cooperate. You are expected to set a standard both in the amount and in the quality of the work you do, just as you need to teach a representative selection of classes, both good and bad. In short, you have to lead from the front.

If, for example, you are developing a programme of classroom observation and support in the department, your door must be the first to be open. If you want to inspire your team with the confidence to admit when they are having problems, you must first be willing to discuss problems that you yourself are facing. This is not an easy thing to do. You need to be open and confident in the way you handle things, and avoid the impression that you are taking the chance to offload your problems.

7   *Be considerate in your handling of other people*

It may seem obvious, but the maxim should be to treat other people as you would wish to be treated yourself. Other people have wishes and needs; do not let your own preferences dominate – as a Head of Department it can be easy to fall into this trap. Do not expect people to drop what they are doing to fit into your plans. Consult your team before you programme a team activity, so that you can choose a time and date which suits the majority (even if it is not the most convenient date for you).

8   *Treat your team evenly and avoid favouritism*

It is usually not sound policy to depend too much on one member of your team. Certainly you must avoid leaving anyone out. On matters to do with team activity (as opposed to individual professional development matters) avoid telling one team member things that you are not prepared to tell them all. Be particularly careful how you allocate teaching groups; the criteria for the allocation should be clear to everyone. Avoid the situation where one person ends up with more than a fair share of the 'challenging' groups.

9   *Listen to what people say*

One of the most damning indictments of any manager is that people say about him or her 'he's so full of himself and what he wants to do, that he never stops to listen to us'. The ability to listen carefully and, where necessary, sympathetically, is an important skill for any manager. You will need to listen properly both to individuals, and to the mood of a meeting.

Beware of always wanting to have the last word, even if you are sure that you are right! When other people are talking, make sure that you give them your full attention. Show that you have listened carefully to what they have wanted to say – if necessary clarify any points about which you are not absolutely sure. If after listening you need to state an alternative view, make sure that you give your reasons clearly, so that you answer any points that others have made.

It is important that you are accessible to people who might want to talk with you. It does not have to be at the precise moment someone mentions something to you – if necessary arrange another time that suits you both and when you will have enough time, preferably that day and certainly not too far ahead. It is not discourteous to ask someone how much time they think they need, so that you can arrange a sensible time to meet and talk – and remember, things usually take longer than people estimate. Being willing to give up time to help people is an important aspect of management responsibility.

10   *Smile and encourage!*
Always give credit where it is due, and always go out of your way to give praise when it is deserved. Make it clear that you appreciate the difficulties people have faced in doing something. It is often a good idea to make the praise specific – 'I really like that because . . .'.

'We slog our guts out and never get any thanks' is far too common a lament in all organisations. Remember, *always* thank people who have done things for you or for the team. If you are negative or grudging you will lose the support of members of your team. People need what have been called 'positive strokes' – praise, thanks, attention. Positive strokes help to build up morale and confidence, and they make people feel that the work they do is appreciated and worthwhile.

Above all, never blame others for your own mistakes. Too many managers are prepared to offload the blame on to others when things go badly, but are happy to take all the credit when things go well – do not join this unhappy band!

In summary, these are the key qualities needed in managing people:

- Communication
- Clarity
- Concern
- Interest
- Appreciation
- Encouragement
- Support

Managing people up, down and sideways

In practice it is not only the people in your particular team with whom you have to work. You will also be working with, and managing, colleagues who are your equals or superiors in the school hierarchy. Managing up and sideways demands particular skills.

As a last resort, in your own team, you can use the right to tell people how things will operate. When working with people outside your team, and particularly when you want something from senior management, you will only succeed if you are persuasive and assertive. The next section deals with the idea of assertive behaviour. The key thing to bear in mind, as you read the section, is that there is a vital difference between 'assertive' and 'aggressive' behaviour.

What is meant by assertive behaviour?

The ideas in this section are based on the work of Claus Moler, although plenty has been written elsewhere on assertiveness. We recognise that we can only outline some of the main ideas in such a short section. And, as with any theory, it is 'easier said than done'. To develop assertiveness you will need to work at it and to learn from your experiences. Imagine the following situations:

Situation 1
You are having a department meeting. At a previous meeting everyone agreed that each team member would prepare an outline for one of the units of work in the new Second Year syllabus. Now you ask everyone which units they would like to work on, so that

ideas can be discussed at the meeting in a fortnight's time. John, however, announces, somewhat aggressively, that he is not going to have time to do it, as he's involved in the school play.

You could react by saying one of these things:

- *I thought we had all agreed, but I suppose if you are really busy. . . . I hadn't realised you were involved in the play. . . . Well, why don't you just leave it this time, John.* This would be *submissive* behaviour on your part. You are reacting defensively, and trying to defuse the situation by avoiding any possible confrontation.
- *Oh come on John, you must have known about the play when we all agreed to do this at the last meeting. We are all busy – I've got the report to the governors to do.* This would be *aggressive* behaviour on your part. You are responding by attacking, implying that John is making more of it than he should.
- *Yes I see your problem, John. It's a busy time of term isn't it? We do need to get this done though, as we did agree that it was a major priority for the department. What about if you just sketched out some ideas in rough for us for the next meeting, and we could put some flesh on the bones at the meeting?* This would be *assertive* behaviour on your part. You have recognised that John has a genuine problem, but you have also, without being aggressive, set it in the context of agreed priorities. Finally you have suggested an alternative approach which goes some way to meeting the needs of both sides.

To be submissive in this sort of situation means that you are neglecting the needs of the task and the team, by allowing an individual need to dominate. To be aggressive may well result in the other person reacting by further aggression or by taking up a position from which it would be difficult to compromise. The assertive response keeps the situation neutral – it focuses on issues rather than personalities, it keeps the door open by offering a positive suggestion which will go some way to meeting all three needs.

Situation 2
All Heads of Department receive this note from the deputy head: 'There have been complaints about unauthorised room changes, which make it difficult to find staff or pupils in an emergency.

The procedure is that I need to know all room changes at least a day in advance.'

Your difficulty is that quite often there are short-notice room changes in your department, as you only have one classroom with blackout. It really would be both difficult and inefficient if you or your team had to notify the deputy a day in advance.

What could you say to the deputy when you see him next?

A submissive answer would be: '*It really would be rather difficult to do it, but I suppose we could try.*'

An aggressive answer would be: '*It just isn't possible. We need to make room changes all the time, and we can't possibly let you know a day in advance. I don't think you know the implications of what you are asking.*'

An assertive answer would be: '*Yes, I can see your difficulty. Let me tell you about the problem from our point of view, and perhaps we can work something out that is going to suit us both.*'

Assertive behaviour is halfway between being submissive and aggressive. Assertive behaviour is when you stand up for your own rights or views, but without detracting from other people's rights or views. Assertiveness aims at achieving an honest, open and direct expression of your own point of view, which at the same time shows that you understand the other person's position. If you, and the members of your team, can behave assertively, the team will be well on its way to highly effective operation.

Here are four ways of expressing yourself assertively.

1 State your rights – with a straightforward statement that stands up for your rights by stating your needs or views clearly and reasonably, eg *Hang on a moment, let me have my say*; *I'm sorry, I would like to help, but I simply don't have time.*

2 Ask the other person – with a straightforward question designed to clarify where the other person stands, or what he/she wants or needs, eg *What is the problem as you see it? What would you like me to do?*

3 Understand both views – show that you do appreciate the other person's view, while at the same time stating your own needs, eg *I can see your point, but . . .*; *I do realise that you are not happy about this, and . . . .*

4 State the effects of behaviour – with a statement that openly explains the adverse effect a person's behaviour is having on you. This is the strongest form of assertion and should be tried

only when necessary, eg *You keep interrupting me, and it is not helping our discussion*; *Please don't raise your voice, it is making us both tense.*

Recognising different behaviours

1   *Submissive*
People behaving submissively are likely to:

- make long, rambling statements (often justifying themselves)
- avoid making 'I' statements, or qualify them, eg *It's only my opinion, but . . .*
- put themselves down, eg *I keep trying but . . .*; *I seem to be hopeless at this*; *Would you mind very much . . .?*
- use phrases that make it easier for others to ignore their needs, eg *It's not important really*; *It doesn't really matter, but . . .*; *I only meant*; *Never mind . . .*
- avoid making eye contact

"People behaving submissively are likely to . . ."
"People behaving aggressively are likely to . . ."

2   *Aggressive*

People behaving aggressively are likely to:

- make excessive use of 'I' statements
- state their opinions as facts, eg *That's rubbish*; *That won't work*
- put other people down, eg *You must be joking! That's stupid . . . That's only your opinion . . .*
- make much use of words like *ought, must, should, have to*
- use aggressive hand gestures
- raise their voice more than necessary
- use sarcasm

3   *Assertive*

People behaving assertively are likely to:

- make statements that are brief and to the point
- use well-considered 'I' statements, eg *I'd like . . . I hope . . . I believe*
- distinguish clearly between fact and opinion, eg *In my experience . . . My opinion is . . . As I see it . . .*
- use open-ended questions to find out what others think or want, eg *How does this affect you? What are your thoughts on . . .*
- look for ways to resolve problems, eg *How can we get around that? How about . . .? What would happen if . . .?*
- keep eye contact without trying to stare down
- speak clearly, neither too loud nor too soft
- appear calm and relaxed

Case Study 9.1:   *For action*
SOME PEOPLE MANAGEMENT ISSUES

A   He scores off us all the time

From a conversation with Susan Barnes in the Creative Arts Faculty:

'I know that John has always been the same, but I find his

manner both unpleasant and unprofessional. I am sure he is a good, even charismatic, teacher himself, but he is not the only good teacher in the school, or even in the department, yet he is always belittling what any of us do in comparison to his own efforts.

He does this to other staff and in front of the pupils. If he comes into my classroom he always finds something to criticise. He does this in front of the pupils, and it undermines my authority. He is so sarcastic about what I am doing. I have a lot of difficult classes and I have come to dread his coming into my room for anything. If I have to send a difficult pupil to him, he seems to ally with the pupil and makes it appear that the pupil would be perfectly alright if only John himself were teaching him, or that I am being unreasonable. Surely it is the job of the Head of Department to support his team . . .'

1   *What does this example indicate about John's perception of his role as Head of Department?*
2   *On the basis of the information you have, analyse this issue.*
3   *If Susan came to you for advice, how would you suggest she tries to tackle the problem?*

B   We all need positive stroking

From a conversation with Joanne Higgs in the Music Department:

'I find it very difficult to work so hard and yet receive no praise or real encouragement for my efforts. Philip is a very good Head of Department in many ways, very hard working himself, always ready to explain things, and he has been very kind to me on a number of occasions, but his standards are extremely high and so are his expectations of people. I have done absolutely everything he has asked and I really do think that I have done rather well, but he seems unable to tell me this although he likes it when I praise something he has done. On the other hand he is very quick to tell me that I have made a mess of things. He can be very critical of other people's performance and he is often very sharp with them. He is usually right in what he says, but he does upset me . . .'

1 *Analyse the people management issue involved in this case study.*
2 *Is there any way that Joanne could try to improve what she perceives as her difficult situation?*

C She makes waves all the time

Fiona Bruce (Head of English) talking to Vivienne Michael (Head of Social Science Faculty):

'I know Priscilla doesn't mean any harm. Her work with the Third Form really has been very good. I know that she has put in a lot of extra work with 3X to prepare them for the drama competition, but she does grumble so much about everything, and her voice is extremely penetrating – nobody can miss hearing. Really she doesn't mean most of it. It's just her way, but people don't realise this, and it does not make her popular with a lot of other staff. She says she just likes to let her feelings out.

Because Priscilla is so loud it makes everybody think that the English Department is having more problems than it really is, and Vera, who still has not really accepted not getting the HoD post herself, uses Priscilla's interventions to suggest to people that I haven't organised things properly yet again. I've tried to ignore it, but it is difficult as it makes so many waves. What do you think I should do?'

1 *Analyse the issue, and advise Fiona.*

D The team have not accepted me

Sunniti Pattni (newly appointed Head of Third Year) is asking advice from Nigel North (Head of Fourth Year):

'I am delighted of course to have got the job. I really didn't expect to beat Philip at the interview. I am worried about a number of things, and because we have always worked well together, I have come to you for advice.

Philip still seems to be very aggrieved about not getting the post, and is not being at all co-operative. He is very slighting about everything I suggest. I suspect that he also resents my being a woman, and an Asian – though of course this is not mentioned.

The year team has worked together for a long time and is very set in its ways. My methods are somewhat differnt from Mr Marshall's. My whole approach is less formal. I want to consult about things and give everyone a chance to air his or her views. I am not at all sure how to tackle this problem. We are due to have our first year meeting next week so that we can prepare for next term when I take over as Year Head.'

1 a) *Clarify the management issue here.*
   b) *If you were Nigel North what advice would you give Sunniti Pattni?*
2 *If you were in Sunniti's position, how would you go about:*
   a) *Tackling the problem with Philip Mackenzie, your 'uncooperative' Deputy Head of Year?*
   b) *Preparing for, and organising, your first year meeting?*

Chapter 10
Building Your Team

We trained hard – but it seemed that every time we were beginning to form up into teams we would be reorganised. I was to learn later in life that we tend to meet any new situation by reorganising and a wonderful method it can be for creating the illusion of progress while producing confusion, inefficiency and demoralisation.

Gaius Petronius 1BC

What is a team?

A team is a group of people who work or relate in a way which helps them to achieve their common objective. In an effective team, team spirit has to be created so that the members work for the benefit of the group. To achieve its task the group needs each member, and so it is in the interests of the group to develop the skills of each member. Back-biting and gossip causes team members to hold back on their performance, and the task is not well achieved. Good individuals do not automatically make a good team until they learn to operate as one.

(David Trethowan, *Teamwork in Schools*,
The Industrial Society)

A team is a group of people who can effectively tackle any task that it is set up to do. 'Effectively' means that the quality of the task accomplishment is the best achievable within the time available, and makes full and economic use of the resources

*available to the team. The contribution drawn from each member
is of the highest possible and one that could not be drawn into
play other than in a context of a supportive team.*
(Everard and Morris, *Effective School Management*)

A great deal has been written about the development and
management of teams in schools. In industry companies spend a
lot of time, effort and money in putting together teams they hope
will work well.

Why are teams so important? There is now so much research
evidence that we can be in no doubt that a good team is the most
effective way of harnessing the efforts of individuals. In any
organisation people find it more satisfying to work in teams; their
performance is improved by working with others in a team; and
the overall objectives of the organisation can best be achieved by
people operating in teams. The idea that most nearly sums this up
is *synergy* – where the total output of a group is greater than the
sum of the output of each individual. In other words,

$$1 + 1 + 1 + 1 = 5$$

There is a vital proviso to all this. A collection of individuals
working together is not necessarily a team. Indeed a bad team may
be both ineffective and destructive of the efforts of the individuals
in the group. The key point we are making in this chapter is that
teams have to be built – they do not just happen.

The good team checklist

If working in a good team is the most effective way of using the
effort and skills of individuals, then the first objective must be to
establish what makes a good team. The list that follows elaborates
on some of the ideas we have already touched on, and introduces
some characteristics of a good team.

An effective team . . .

1 Shares clear objectives and agreed goals
   - agrees on what the team is trying to do and its priorities for
     action
   - agrees on what differences are tolerable within the team
   - clarifies the roles of team members
   - discusses values and reaches a general consensus on the
     underlying philosophy of the team

2   Has clear procedures
   - for holding meetings
   - for making decisions
   - for delegating responsibility

3   Reviews its progress regularly
   - reassesses its objectives
   - evaluates the processes the team is using
   - does not spend too much time dissecting the past

4   Has leadership appropriate to its membership
   - the leader is visible and accessible
   - the leader utilises the strengths of all the team members
   - the leader models the philosophy of the team

5   Has open lines of communication
   - team members talk to each other about issues, and not just to the team leader
   - recognises each person's contribution
   - gives positive and negative feedback
   - people are open-minded to other people's arguments
   - welcomes ideas and advice from outside the team
   - people are skilled in sending and receiving messages in face-to-face communication

6   Has a climate of support and trust
   - people give and ask for support
   - team members spend enough time together to function effectively
   - team members' strengths are used and built upon
   - there is respect for other people's views
   - relates positively to other teams and groups

7   Recognises that conflict is inevitable and can be constructive
   - issues are dealt with immediately and openly
   - people are assertive
   - feelings are recognised and dealt with
   - people are encouraged to contribute ideas
   - conflicting viewpoints are seen as normal, and dealt with constructively

8   Is concerned with the personal and career development of its members
   - regular reviews are carried out with each team member

- the leader looks for opportunities to develop each member
- members look for opportunities to develop other members
- members look for opportunities to develop their team leader

At first reading this checklist may seem a long, and perhaps, idealistic, outline of what a good team needs to have and be. It would be fair to say that there are not many teams which display all these characteristics. A team can be effective even if it does not score ten-out-of-ten for everything. What the checklist does provide, however, is a set of targets against which a team can review its progress – something that all good teams do!

Figure 10a shows how the ideas on the checklist can be summarised:

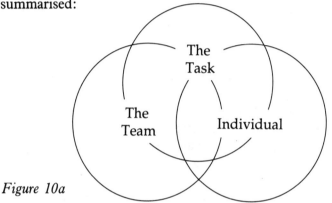

Figure 10a

An effective team needs to meet three distinct, yet closely linked, sets of needs. Those of the task; the team; and of the individuals.

1 Task needs
To achieve its *task* the team has to focus on questions such as What? Why? How? Who? How well did we do? The task need focuses on the way the team establishes priorities, sets objectives, plans and implements actions, reviews progress.

2 Team needs
In order to achieve its task, the *team* itself has to meet its own needs. As we said before, teams need to be built and maintained, they do not just happen when a group of people are asked to do something together. The team need focuses on creating openness and trust, clarifying team roles, resolving conflicts, setting shared objecties.

3   *Individual needs*
It is vital to remember that, although they work as a team, the team is composed of *individuals* who will have needs which may or may not be connected with the team as a whole. The individual need focuses on the respect for different viewpoints, the recognition of feelings, the use of individuals' particular strengths, and the need for individuals to develop themselves for life after the team.

The role of the team leader

As a middle manager you have been made the leader of a team – it may be a subject department or faculty, a group of form tutors, or a curriculum initiative involving colleagues from a number of departments. Whichever it is, your team will consist of a group of individuals who have been brought together to carry out a common task – in the case of a department, to plan and deliver the teaching of that subject.

As a team leader you will play a crucial role in building the team, and then in maintaining its effectiveness. Some of this team building work will be high-profile and visible, but much of it will be behind the scenes, self-effacing work that receives no recognition and often little credit – your reward will be the private knowledge that without such work the team would not be so effective.

In the checklist earlier in the chapter it was suggested that style of leadership needed to be appropriate to the particular team. There is no blueprint for how to build and lead a team, and so the ideas that follow are guidelines only, which you will need to adapt and modify to match your particular situation.

Building the team

The first point to make is that to build an effective team may take quite some time. Some teams gel more quickly than others, while some teams never really develop to their potential, and a few teams are a disaster from start to finish.

Experience from a range of different types of organisations suggests that team development typically displays four stages:

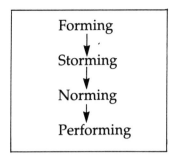

Forming is the initial stage in which the team is put together. Commercial organisations use a battery of aptitude and personality tests to help them put together teams which are likely to be effective. In school, if you are a Head of Department or Head of Year, you are unlikely to enjoy that luxury, as you may well inherit an existing team. Over time, however, you may have the opportunity to influence the composition of your team as its composition changes.

At the *storming* stage a team is characterised by tensions as team members jockey for position. If you are a new team leader there may well be considerable mistrust of your motives and actions. At this stage team leader actions may be dominated by telling, either because other people are unwilling to contribute much, or because cooperation is low.

Once through the storming, the *norming* stage is when the team begins to weld together. Relations between some team members may still be somewhat formal, and disagreements and conflicts may remain hidden. At this stage the leader can begin to delegate more, as the roles of team members are sorted out and as tensions decrease.

The *performing* stage represents the target for the team's style of operating. This stage is characterised by a high level of trust and support among team members, and by an openness in discussion that is not achieved at other stages. Conflicts and disagreements are brought into the open and resolved. The strengths of team members are recognised and used by the team to achieve its objectives. The team is confident enough to be self-critical and accept and use outside advice.

Many teams go through all four stages in their building process, quite a few never reach the latter stages, and a fortunate few jump through the early stages quickly to reach full potential. In the remainder of this chapter we look at some of the elements that you might consider at the various stages.

Forming

Whatever sort of team you are going to lead, as a middle manager you are not likely to have a lot of say over its composition. If you take over a department or year team, most of its members will already be in post. If you are given leadership of a cross-curricular initiative – PSE, Technology, Integrated Studies etc – it is likely that the team membership will be largely determined by circumstances and the senior management. Thus your task is to weld together a team from a group of people you have not selected yourself.

The ways that you can best set about this task will depend on a number of variables, such as the size of the team, the nature of the team task, the personalities involved, and the time you have available. Thus it is not possible to suggest any hard and fast rules about team building; what you do need to bear in mind are the general points we made about managing people in the previous chapter.

Case Study 10.1 outlines a variety of approaches to team building which could be tried with a team that has either been recently formed, or which has some new personnel. The second case study analyses in detail some of the issues involved in forming a team that is experiencing particular difficulties.

Case Study 10.1: *For*
IDEAS FOR TEAM BUILDING *reflection*

At a middle management training course a group of teachers brainstormed these ideas for building 'team spirit'.

- Positive talks – one to one
- Discussion of allocation of responsibilities within the department
- Meals at Head of Department's house
- Refreshments at team meetings

- Supply of 'goodies' to each teacher, for use in the classroom
- Taking part in social team games with other departments
- Setting own standards and expectations
- Review of department's aims and objectives
- Sessions to share ideas for classroom activities
- Daily department notices
- Revolving the chair at meetings
- Financial delegation in support of delegated team roles
- Departmental logo – on memo slips, etc.
- Praising people in public
- Cheese and wine at the end of term
- Making other people aware of team members' achievements
- Show real interest in people's lives (without being intrusive)
- Keys! – open access to department areas for all team members

Many of the points made by these teachers are reflected in the previous chapter on managing people; for example, the need for the team leader to spend time with and to get to know the members of the team, the need for regular and clear communication, the need for praise and recognition of effort and good work. What also emerges from this list is a desire to establish a team identity through things like a department logo, and through socialisation – social sessions and food are mentioned quite a lot! The important element of agreeing responsibilities and delegation is also mentioned, and later in this chapter we look in more detail at delegation.

Case Study 10.2:   *For*
BUILDING A TEAM – LEADING FROM BELOW *reflection*

This case study examines a situation in which middle managers find themselves from time to time – leading a team of people, the majority of whom are senior to the team leader. Such a situation always creates particular challenges, and demands very high order team leadership.

From a discussion between Meriel Hemmings and Vivienne Michaels. Meriel is requesting advice . . .

'I was very pleased when Mrs Gatlin asked me to take responsibility for introducing CPVE into the Sixth Form. It's an exciting initiative and I really believe it has a lot to offer our Sixth Form and that we could develop it into a very attractive course. Then Mrs Perkins told me which staff she was allocating to the team and I began to get worried. They seem to regard CPVE as a place where they can offload senior staff, who have to do some teaching, but who want to avoid a heavy marking commitment. On my team I have one Deputy Head, two Senior Teachers, the Head of Business studies, the Head of Classics and Mrs Rossiter. I have never had a promoted post before and I am only getting an A Grade allowance for this task. How am I meant to lead so many senior people? I was sufficiently worried to go to see Mrs Gatlin, but she only laughed and said, 'Well, dear, you will have to lead from below.'

The reality turned out to be even worse than I had feared. Seniority does not necessarily go hand in hand with enthusiasm or ability.

Mr Brown (Deputy Head Pastoral) is supportive in theory, but in practice he is always too busy to attend the team meetings and often fails to turn up at the lessons at all. Luckily I am timetabled to teamteach with him some of the time, so I just teach the lessons for him. When I do catch up with him, he is totally preoccupied with crises thrown up by the pastoral system and hasn't the time to listen to me at all. He really thinks it's my job to tell the team what to do – giving out a list of duties every Monday morning, just like he does for the Year Tutors.

Mrs Gibbs (Senior teacher) is extremely conscientious and anxious to do her share. Unfortunately she has not been on a course or read a book for years. She is totally out of touch and when it is her turn to produce an assignment, she brings out worksheets, which, I am sure, she must have had in the cupboard for years. They are out of date and totally unsuitable and, just to add to my troubles, they are racist and sexist as well, and the children pick this up immediately. It is very embarrassing for us all and gentle hints don't seem to have any effect. I don't know how to tell her and whether, if I did, she would understand sufficiently to be able to change her ways. Another problem is that, like Mr Brown, she sometimes fails to turn up for lessons, especially when she is timetabled to team teach with me – so I am team teaching on my own!

Mr Wade (Senior teacher) should be an asset. He is both capable and creative, but CPVE is about bottom of his list of priorities and, to be fair to him, he has made this quite plain. He understands all the issues, but has made it clear that he has no intention of increasing his own input to compensate for the deficiencies of the others. He will produce an assignment when his turn comes up, but no more. The infuriating thing is that his assignments are very good indeed, but it is like getting blood out of a stone.

Mr Phillips (Head of Business Studies) should be dealing with all the IT but it is becoming apparent that although he thinks he is a whizz kid, he is not in fact as knowledgeable about computing as he would have us believe. He has made some nasty mistakes, which revealed how superficial his expertise really is. This means that he is not really suitable to help the rest of the team learn how to use computers as part of their assignments. More serious still, when I have had to mention a problem to him, he has been quite rude to me. He does not like me telling him what to do and is much nastier about this than the really senior staff.

I know why they put **Miss Cline** (Head of Classics) on the team. With falling rolls, there is no way that they could give her a full timetable of Classics. She does not regard CPVE as an academic subject or see why she should change her teaching style. Team teaching is a major threat to her independence. She really does not like anyone in the classroom with her. Her assignments are much too academic and she persists in telling the group what the correct answer is, because that is so important to her perception of how you should teach.

Mrs Rossiter comes in three days a week to teach Home Economics. It is another area of the curriculum where numbers are contracting and there was slack on her timetable, so she was attached to the team. She had never heard of CPVE but is perfectly happy to be part of the team, provided that I tell her what to do, because she thinks that it is 'nice' for the pupils to be able to do some cooking. I would really like her to take on liaison with the FE college, as quite a number of them do the catering option, but she tends to get very worried about things and I feel it would be unfair on both sides to ask her. She is obsessed with trivial detail and is forever asking me to explain things. As assignments are ongoing through the week and each teacher is meant to continue from whatever point the group has reached at that moment, simply telling her what to do next is taking up a lot of my time.

Quite frankly, I am at my wits' end to know what to do about them . . .'

With such a difficult problem it was essential that Meriel should stand back from the situation and try to clarify the issues, before she thought about possible courses of action. Vivienne therefore advised Meriel that she should use our approach to problem solving and offered to help her work it through.

1 Clarification

What is the problem? – Meriel is finding it very difficult to build a CPVE team from the staff she has been allocated.

Does it have component parts? – Too many senior staff. Members of the team have other priorities. Lack of commitment to the team. Lack of the right expertise.

What are the symptoms? – Little useful input by members of the team. Meriel is having to do too much work herself.

2 Analyse the issues

Leading from below – Meriel has to establish herself as the leader, in a situation where almost all the members of the team are senior to her in status.

Establishing the status of her project – recognition of CPVE as an important element in the Sixth Form curriculum. Putting senior staff on the team could have done a lot to help the status of the project, but they do not think CPVE is important enough to attend planning meetings and their attitude has accentuated the problem.

Developing the team – Meriel will need to think of ways of developing her team. The staff have been allocated to CPVE. Meriel was given no opportunity to select her team, nor are they volunteers. She therefore has to enthuse her team in order to build up commitment to the project. She also has to build up the skills of most of the members of the team so that they can make a more valuable input.

3   Approaches (generate ideas and discuss possible strategies)

a)   *Change the team*
Vivienne and Meriel realised that they could not start from the obvious premise that the team was unsuitable and that changes in personnel needed to be made. Going to the Head and saying that you wanted to remove a Deputy Head and several senior colleagues from your team, because they lacked the right expertise and did not turn up for meetings, was not a viable strategy. This move would create a lot of ill-feeling and the Head would be likely to say to Meriel that it was not that the team was no good, but that Meriel had failed as a manager.

This meant that they had to consider ways of improving the situation with the existing team – at least for the time being. Establishing her leadership role seemed to be the crucial issue, so Meriel and Vivienne began to examine ways to achieve this objective.

b)   *Training for Meriel*
One of the problems was that Meriel was not experienced as a team leader or in running meetings. Vivienne suggested that because she was having to deal with some difficult personalities and issues, assertiveness training might be helpful for Meriel. This would show her ways of getting the team to listen to what she wanted to say without her sounding either aggressive or impolite. Training videos were available through the local Teachers' Centre, which twice a year ran a course of this nature. This could perhaps be followed up with more specific management training, which could help to develop her team.

c)   *Follow up lapses*
Vivienne felt it imperative that the problem of absence from

meetings or lessons be addressed as this affected the whole status of the subject. She argued that it was a mistake for Meriel to continue to teach the others' lessons for them and that this made a travesty of the whole idea of team teaching. She suggested monitoring attendance so that Meriel had a record of exactly what was happening – this would help the others appreciate the seriousness of the problem. 'They probably don't realise that they are doing it so often,' she said. It would also provide a safeguard in case any parents complained or Meriel had to justify her actions to the Head. After all, senior staff should set the rest of the team an example of good practice and Mrs Gatlin, the Head, would not be happy if she knew what was happening.

Meriel would have to see each member of staff who missed a lesson or meeting. It was acceptable that in a crisis a very senior member of staff might have to miss the occasional session, but it was unacceptable that this should be happening frequently and this point needed to be established. It was also unacceptable that Mr Brown or Mrs Gibbs should consistently fix meetings with parents when they should be teaching CPVE. As team leader Meriel had the right to know why a lesson had been missed and what the member of staff meant to do about it. It would be difficult at first but persistence would be likely to pay off. (At the very least they were likely to fix their interviews with parents at a time when they were meant to be teaching some other subject.) The important thing was to carry out this sensitive task as pleasantly and as positively as possible. (This is why assertiveness training would be helpful.) She must not sound aggrieved or as if she were accusing a member of the team of negligence, but it was important for the morale of the whole team that Meriel was seen to tackle this problem.

d)   *Try to build on strengths*
There were at least two members of the team who were willing to contribute, although they needed direction, and one member who already produced good assignments. These were strengths on which Meriel could build. There was a chance that if Mr Wade saw Meriel was taking steps to tackle the problem of dealing with the deficiencies of the team he might be persuaded to give her some support. She needed to talk frankly to him.

e) *Improve assignment writing*

The quality of the work produced by some members of the team was a problem which needed urgent attention. Mrs Gibbs, Miss Cline and Mr Phillips would have to be told that the assignments that they were producing at present did not meet CPVE requirements and were likely to be rejected by the course moderator. In rejecting their work Meriel would need to stress that assignment writing for CPVE was different in nature from the kind of worksheets produced in the past for courses such as BTEC and that examples of good practice and training in how to write assignments would be provided for the team.

f) *Provide INSET*

The team clearly needed INSET. How to design suitable assignments and use of computers in the classroom, were obvious areas. This would also provide opportunities for the CPVE staff to work together as a team and would help team development. Meriel would need to bid for a sizeable share of the school's allowance. As she is developing a new course which will involve a large number of pupils she has a good case for this bid. The local Teachers' Centre was also likely to be running some courses to support CPVE since the LEA was giving this initiative a high profile. She might also be able to run some joint INSET with neighbouring schools. Working with other people who were involved in CPVE might help Meriel's team.

g) *Stop doing their jobs for them*

This followed on from what Vivienne had said about team teaching. If Meriel went on doing all the work herself, she would only tire herself out and she would not have created a team. Giving Mrs Rossiter liaison with the FE college was actually a good idea, which should be tried, even if she needed a lot of direction at first. It would help Mrs Rossiter to understand better the nature of the CPVE course.

Who can help with the solution?

Talking the problem through with a colleague who had had several years' experience of leading and developing a team was useful for Meriel as it helped her to distinguish the issues from the personalities. (Vivienne was an experienced Head of Faculty.)

Mr Wade could clearly help her. This was why she had to demonstrate to him that she was worth helping.

She could bring in appropriate advisers to talk to the team about CPVE and to lead some of the INSET.

As CPVE was a one-year course it would be a sensible move to book an appointment with Mrs Perkins (the Deputy Head who dealt with the timetable) fairly soon in order to discuss next year's team, so that Meriel could take the initiative in suggesting suitable people. She must not belittle the existing team in any way, nor attempt to remove them all, but this could be a way of bringing in some more suitable people next time round.

4　Action

Some of the suggestions generated above were short-term solutions and some were more long-term solutions. Meriel and Vivienne therefore had to decide in what order she should do things. The management issues such as asserting her authority as team leader and ensuring attendance etc had to be implemented immediately, whereas the training and INSET would have to form part of a programme of activities which would continue over the year. Vivienne agreed that she would continue to provide support for Meriel by having a session with her once a month to review the position and evaluate progress.

Staff selection

Selecting people for a team is a vital element in the team-forming process, but, as we have already suggested, being in a position to select is not a luxury afforded to many middle managers. The one time a Head of Department does get the opportunity to participate in the selection of staff is when a member of the department leaves.

The way the school organises and conducts its staff selection is not your responsibility – that is the province of the Head and governors. Nevertheless, if someone is being appointed to your team, you can make an important contribution. If you are not invited to be involved in the procedure, do not be afraid to ask. You cannot demand the right to be consulted, but you certainly want to establish your interest – it is one of the few opportuities you will have to create the kind of team you want.

As a middle manager you might be involved in staff selection at some or all of three stages – before, on the day, and at the interviews. There are three common faults which tend to lead to the wrong people being selected, and it is worth bearing these in mind right from the start.

1 *Before* The people involved in the selection procedure are not sufficiently clear about the kind of person, in terms of qualities or experience, who is being sought for the post.

2 *On the day* Judgements about candidates are made too quickly and based on superficial elements, such as looks, voice, or mannerisms.

3 *At the interview* Candidates are not asked the right questions in the right way to allow really informed judgements about selection to be made.

Ten steps in staff selection

The proof of the effectiveness of any selection process is not only in the quality of the staff built up over time, but also in the extent to which one gets surprises. In the ideal situation a selector should get a good idea at the end of the day of the kind of person she is getting and it is useful to review notes made during or immediately after the interview six months later to see how far the picture of the person appointed was an accurate one.

(Joan Dean, *Managing the Secondary School*, 1986)

1 *Decide what you want*
Think out carefully what you want. It is important to have clear ideas about how you see your department developing in the future, and staff selection is your way through to this. Do you want to replace the person who is leaving with someone with similar skills and abilities, or do you want to use the opportunity to make radical changes to the composition and roles of your team?

2 *Draw up a job description*
When you are clear about what you want, you are ready to draw

up the job description. The Head will probably ask you to draft this out. You need to describe the job: its purpose is, what teaching is involved and what the responsibilities of the post are. An accurate job description will help you attract the kind of candidate you want. Two examples are given in Case Study 10.4.

3   Construct a person specification
The person specification describes the person wanted to fill this particular vacancy. Some LEAs still use a combined job description and person specification, but increasingly they are seen as separate documents. The job description is sent out to applicants and the person specification is used by the interviewers to help them in their task of selecting the most suitable candidate. The kinds of thing you are expected to include in a person specification are:

a) Qualifications. Is a graduate needed? What particular know-ledge, skills or abilities are needed?
b) Experience. Does the applicant need experience of GCSE or A Level teaching? Is it important that she or he has taught in a school that is similar to yours in organisation?
c) Broad age range: Is it a first post or is experience required?
d) Special requirements: eg a firm commitment to mixed ability teaching or to a multicultural approach, or a willingness to contribute to extra-curricular activities.

4   Advertise the post
The Head may consult you when drawing up the advertisement. Although some LEAs use job advertisements to highlight LEA priorities and leave little space for details of the actual post, the purpose of the advertisement should be to attract suitable applicants to apply for the post. The advertisement should briefly encapsulate the information given in the job description and give a clear impression of what is required.

Figure 10b shows a typical advertisement.

5   Analyse the applications
Usually the Head will suggest that you read the application forms and the candidates' references and will ask your opinion. The way that the candidate has filled in the form will indicate what she or he thinks is important and how she or he organises material. This

BESTHAMPTON EDUCATION AUTHORITY

Bestwick Park School, Bestwick Park Avenue,
Besthampton PLJ 134

Required for September 19..
Teacher of Craft Technology, Main Professional Grade.
An A Grade responsibility allowance could be available for a
suitable candidate, though new entrants to the profession will
be considered.
The successful candidate will be required to teach
Technology throughout the school in a well-established and
lively department, with large examination classes. An interest
in curriculum development and establishing links with industry
would be an advantage, as TVEI is being introduced into the
school in September.

Application forms and further details of the post may be obtained
from the Headteacher at the school, and should be returned
within 14 days.

Figure 10b

will make a favourable or unfavourable initial impression on you,
but it is a good idea to follow this by using a checklist or a grid to
help you evaluate the candidates and to see whether they fulfil the
job description and person specification. If you offer this to the
Head to support your opinion about the candidates, it demon-
strates that you are using an analytical approach and gives more
weight to your opinion than if you simply say 'I like Mrs X and
want her in my department'. An example of an Evaluation Grid is
given in Case study 10.3.

6   *Read the references and construct a shortlist*
The Head will send for references on the most promising
candidates and is likely to show you these and to ask your opinion
before constructing the final shortlist. Some points to watch out
for:

a) Has the candidate given his or her present Headteacher as one
    of the referees? If not, find out why at some stage in the
    procedure.
b) A reference normally lists all the candidate's good points –
    check how far these fit your list of requirements.

c) Does what the referee say fit what the candidate has said on the application form?

d) Look for the omissions. References should be positive documents, the omissions indicate possible areas of weakness.

The analysis of the application forms and the references will indicate who the front runners are for the post so that you can advise the Head on the drawing up of the shortlist. In many LEAs the Subject Adviser or Local Education Office will also be consulted at this stage. For most teaching posts between four and six candidates are invited for interview.

7   *Prepare the information the candidates will need*
It is a good idea to assemble some information about the department. If you have a department document (see, for example, Case Study 6.4 on page 81) it is a good idea to have that sent to the shortlisted candidates together with a copy of the syllabus, when the information about the interviews is dispatched. That will give candidates time to digest important information about your department which would be hard for them to assimilate on the day. Check that the letter of information sent to the candidates tells them how the day will be organised – the candidates will appreciate knowing this.

8   *On the day*
The time the candidates spend in school should be planned carefully. Every part of the session is an opportunity for getting information from them and giving them information about the school. A good interview should be a two-way process, during which the candidate and the department assess each other and decide whether they want to work together. On the day itself you are likely to be involved in:

a) Providing the candidates with a tour of the school with an emphasis on the teaching area used by your department. This is so that the candidates can see what facilities the department has.

b) Introducing them to the other members of the department so that the team and the candidate have an opportunity to get an impression of each other.

c) A one-to-one session with the candidate. This gives you the opportunity to find out more about the candidate than you can glean from the application form.

9   *Handling the candidates*
a)   Be open and welcoming. They are your guests and you want them to have a good impression of the school even if you do not appoint them.
b)   Encourage them to ask questions.
c)   Take them into classrooms and observe how they react with your pupils.
d)   Think carefully about the way you ask questions so that you get the most out of the candidates. Avoid leading or multi-part questions. Be encouraging, so that the interviewee relaxes and performs well.
e)   Above all, really listen to the answers and pick them up in supplementary questions so that you get beyond the standard or prepared interview answer.

10   *Make the appointment*
You will probably not be a member of the panel at the formal interview; this is conducted by the Head, usually with an Adviser or someone from the local Education Office. It is, however, very likely that the Head will want to consult you at the conclusion of the formal interviews before offering the post to the preferred candidate. Once an offer has been accepted, make sure you congratulate the successful candidate and make arrangements about how to make further contact, eg a follow-up visit to meet the department.

Job descriptions

In most LEAs Heads are required to produce job descriptions, and to agree them with individual members of staff. To do this effectively the Head is likely to ask you, as team leader, to make at least an initial draft.

If you are drawing up a job description prior to a selection process, then the document will be used to help you select the right person, but will need to be discussed with the person appointed. If you are drawing up job descriptions for existing

Case Study 10.3:
EVALUATION GRID FOR ASSESSING JOB APPLICATIONS

POST: Allowance A 2nd in Mod. Lang. Dept.	MEETS REQUIREMENTS			
	Fully	Partially	Not at all	Points scored
Preferred age 25–35				
Graduate				
Experience in school of similar size & composition				
Experience in a large modern department				
Experience of good professional relationships, especially ability to work in a team.				
Evidence of good teaching skills				
Ability to teach German as well as French & Spanish				
Experience of teaching GCSE and A level in at least one language				
Recent experience of Curriculum Development				
Recent experience of INSET (courses)				
Evidence of initiatives which indicate willingness/ability to take responsibility/leadership potential				
Evidence of commitment to LEA's policy priorities (ie improving multicultural content of the dept. syllabus)				
Evidence of participation in extracurricular activities				
Scoring: Each area max. 5 Requirements: ✓ as relevant				

team members you could approach the task in two ways. You could do a first draft and then discuss and agree it with the members of your team, or you could involve team members in the drafting process (possibly as part of your staff development programme). When people are involved in drafting as well as agreeing their job descriptions, the exercise is usually more effective in terms of team building.

A job description usually consists of:

- the job title
- a brief description of the purpose of the job
- a description of the reporting arrangements
- an outline of the main duties/responsibilities involved

The purpose of drawing up a job description is to make clear to both parties what the job should involve. The document, therefore, needs to define responsibilities fairly precisely, or at least as precisely as it is possible to do at the time.

If you are a Head of Department the kind of job description you will be involved in formulating will be either for main scale teachers or for allowance posts, such as a Second in Department. In both cases you will want to define what teaching is required; for example, 'to teach throughout the school', or 'to teach up to and including GCSE', or 'to teach mainly in the lower school'. In many cases the person will also carry some area of specific responsibility which you will need to define; for example, 'to be in charge of timetabled drama', or 'to co-ordinate the work of the First Year Integrated Humanities team', or 'to be responsible, with the Librarian, for the smooth running of the school's library resources'.

Where appropriate it can be useful to put a time scale on tasks that are of a limited duration; for example, 'during this academic year to co-ordinate the development of the new A level course, and to produce a scheme of work for discussion by the department in April/May'.

SOME SAMPLE JOB DESCRIPTIONS

A.　Bestwick Park School. Second in the Physics Department – Grade A

This is a new post in the school, where, in addition to a substantial teaching commitment throughout the school, the post holder will be responsible to the Head of Physics in assisting in the running of the department and will deputise for the Head of Department should he be absent.

Specific duties
1　To have oversight of the Physics part of the Integrated Science Course in the lower school, and of the lower school Physics curriculum.
2　To assist the Head of Faculty in ensuring race and gender equality in the Third Year option choices, particularly in regard to encouraging girls' interest in the Physical Sciences.
3　To liaise with the co-ordinators of CPVE and TVEI on the Science Technology components of these courses, including work experience relevant to such courses.
4　To establish links with local industry.
5　From time to time to carry out additional duties as allocated by the Headteacher.

These duties are to be reviewed and revised as and when appropriate.

B.　Bestwick Park School. Deputy Head of Year – Grade A

The Deputy Head of Year will be responsible for assisting the Head of Year in running the Year Team and dealing with the Year Group in order to ensure the smooth running of the school's pastoral system and will deputise for the Head of Year should she or he be absent.

Specific duties
1　To assist the Year Head in checking that Year Tutors are present.

2   To cover registers when necessary.

3   To check lesson attendance sheets/class registers and to refer any truants or problem cases to the Head of Year.

4   To attend Head of Year meetings.

5   To assist the Head of Year with Parents' Evenings.

6   To assist the Head of Year with collating reports and reply slips.

7   To share the running of Year Detentions with the Year Heads.

8   To assist with enforcing sanctions such as Early Report.

9   To assist with filing and record-keeping as required, eg pupil files, records of case conferences, meetings with parents or outside agencies.

10   To assist the Head of Year in maintaining a good standard of uniform and equipment for their year group, eg through regular uniform or equipment checks.

11   To support the Year Tutors in checking the Homework Link books.

12   From time to time to carry out additional duties as allocated by the Headteacher.

These duties are to be reviewed and revised as necessary.

Storming

Moving to take up a middle management post in a new school, or in your present school, can cause a lot of stress – for you and for the team you take over. It is perfectly normal for a team to go through a storming stage. It is really very common, although that is never much of a comfort if you are suffering from a particularly severe case of storming!

Your new team may seem reserved and not very enthusiastic or cooperative. That is hardly surprising – they don't know you from Adam, and they are taking their time to make judgements about you. Perhaps there are one or two people who thought that they should have been given your job. Their resentment may show at times; it's understandable if they are a little bit dismissive of some of your first ideas. The team you are taking over may well have settled into a routine way of working over the years. They are happy with the way they are doing things, and the last thing they want is some newcomer messing around and changing things. It would be hardly surprising if some members of the team resisted or even undermined any early changes you make.

So our advice is this:

1   Remember that storming is common and perfectly normal.
2   If it happens, you need to work through it as normally as you can – don't over-react.
3   Think carefully about ways you could try to work through the difficulties.
4   Behave as you would want team members to behave – be open and assertive.

Case Study 10.5:   *For action*
A STORMING FIRST YEAR

Simon Tucker was appointed Head of Science at Bestwick Park School, shortly after Mrs Gatlin became Head of the school. One of the things she said to him after the interview was that she wanted 'Science in the school pepped up a bit'.

Science was a leading faculty in the school. A chart of the responsibilities of the three departments which together made up the faculty can be found in the chapter on 'Communications'. This case study focuses upon the relationship between Simon and Helen Trevor, Head of Chemistry, as seen by Simon. He knew that Helen, who had been in the school for some years, had applied for the Head of Faculty post but had not been interviewed.

This account of the problems Simon faced in his first year is taken from a job appraisal session he had that summer with Michael Wade, Senior Teacher responsible for staff development.

At first Helen was rather reserved, but she seemed very helpful. She made a point of reminding me about things that needed doing, and of course she knew where everything in the faculty was. She quite often did things for me, things that were strictly my responsibility – like making out the faculty set lists to give to the office. At first it was very useful, but after a while it began to get on my nerves – it was as if she was trying to prove a point. I let it ride for a while, then I decided that I needed to put a stop to it. So next time that she did something like that – getting some more filing slips printed – I thanked her, but said firmly that I did not want to do things this way in future and it would be better if she consulted me before doing things like this. I think it would be fair to say that she went off in a bit of a huff.

The school's policy was to have department meetings once a month. I wanted to change that for Science but, under the circumstances, not immediately. At our first meeting we spent most of the time discussing course work. The old Head of Department had done nothing on this and I knew that Mrs Gatlin was depending on me to do something about the very traditional and didactic teaching methods used particularly by the Chemistry Department. We all agreed to produce a piece of coursework for the next meeting (Christopher Jones would assist the probationer in his department). Helen agreed upon her topic, although without much outward show of enthusiasm.

It was between this meeting and the next that I picked up odd pieces of staffroom gossip that Helen was complaining to her friends that things were not going well in the department. In fact Mrs Perkins, one of the deputies, made a point of asking how things were going and how I was getting on with Helen. I said, 'Fine'. The talking behind my back really got me down, but there didn't seem to be much I could do about it, so I just left it.

At the next meeting we duly looked at the draft coursework. I decided that it would be best if we looked at mine first. It was hardly anything revolutionary, but I did feel that it should at least be something a bit different, to start as I hoped the faculty would go on. They were all as quiet as mice. Helen said nothing, even when I asked her if she was happy with the groupwork involved. Her answer was simply, 'We've done groupwork before'. So far so good, even if I was doing all the talking.

Next we looked at Helen's coursework. I had asked for copies before the meeting, but I hadn't received any, so this was the first time I had seen it. Frankly it was awful. All I could do was to say vague things like, 'There are some nice ideas here,' and to praise the one bit that was alright. At the end of the meeting I said that I would take away all the drafts, and based on what we had discussed, make a few changes, put them into the format we *needed etc. I thought the only thing to do would be to do a major rewrite on Helen's – I didn't have the nerve to ask her to do again.*

After that things seemed to go along more smoothly. I did have a word with Helen about the coursework and showed her my changes. She did not react to what I had done and seemed to accept the new version. Apart from that I avoided her as much as I could; my thinking was that it was better to let things settle down. My aim was to work at things on my own, things which other people in the department could see were being done – sorting out the resource cupboard, putting up displays in classrooms, etc. Another meeting passed without much incident, although we only really talked about admin.

The big crunch came just before Xmas, when the 4th year did their first practice coursework assessment. We had agreed to use Helen's assignment, or at least my reworking of it. I asked each person to mark five from their set so that I could do some form of internal moderation. Helen had not used the agreed coursework at all. She had given her group what was virtually her original version of the assignment.

I was furious. The next day I put a note in Helen's pigeon hole, asking to see her at the end of school. We had a humdinger of a row. By the end of it we were both shouting until Helen stormed out. I had had enough and went straight to the Head. She was good and calmed me down, and we talked it through. She said that she did not want to intervene yet, as it was up to me to sort it out if I could. I felt a bit let down at the time, but in retrospect I think she was right.

That was the low point of the year for the department. By the end of the year things had got better – they were still not good, but Helen and I were on speaking terms. At the end of the first term, a week or so after the row, I invited all the department out to lunch. It wasn't a relaxed occasion, but I think it helped – I don't know what I would have done if Helen had refused! Next term, on the Head's advice, I asked one of the LEA's advisory teachers to come in and talk to us about coursework assignments. This worked quite well as he was saying much the same as me, but it seemed to have more effect coming from an outsider. After that first practice assignment, I took the opportunity at a faculty meeting to suggest how my own draft coursework should be changed, in the light of our experience. I think this probably helped a bit too.

Looking back on the year, if I could do it over again, I would want to do some things a bit differently. I don't think I could have avoided clashing with Helen at some stage, but it might not have been so traumatic.

I should have been firmer right from the start about doing things which were my responsibility, and I should have had a talk with Helen to sort out some things that I could have delegated to her.

I should have spent more time talking through her first coursework draft – it simply did not work for me to take it away and redo it. I should have made the effort to do it with her even if the end result had not been so good. I should not have avoided Helen during that second half of the first term. I really needed to have made a point of talking to her, and trying to build up a better relationship.

I certainly should not have allowed myself to be provoked into losing my temper when we had the row. I did need to speak with her, but not if I wasn't able to be at least fairly calm. Getting angry like that did more harm than good in the long run.

1   *Do you agree with Simon's analysis?*
2   *With the benefit of detachment, what other strategies might he have used at particular times during the year?*

Strategies for dealing with difficult team members

There are many ways of trying to deal with behaviours that are causing difficulty within the team. It is up to you to decide how you will tackle actual situations, and as in any management problem your first need is to clarify the issues.

Clarifying the issues
1   What does the label 'difficult' really mean? Identify the 'difficult' behaviours being used: What happens? In what circumstances/situations? How often does it happen?
2   Whose problem is it? Describe the effects of the 'difficult' member's behaviour on:
- *Yourself* What feelings does this 'difficult' behaviour produce in you? How do you respond to the 'difficult' behaviour? If you can, try to write down the thoughts that

go along with your response, as these may be clues to your own blocks in changing that behaviour.

- *Other team members* Observe their reactions/behaviour. If possible, find out their feelings.
- *The team task* Can you identify the effect on team objectives? In what ways is the 'difficult' behaviour reducing team effectiveness?
- *The individual* who is producing the difficult behaviour.

3   What would you like to change? How would you like to change behaviours in the team? How can this be done? Consider and investigate reasons for 'difficult' behaviour with the individual concerned. Look at different strategies to help change or control the situation. What about other people's behaviour – yours, or that of other team members – does it need to change?

Once you are as clear as you can be about what the difficulty involves, you can think about how to try and tackle it. Some ideas are briefly outlined in Case study 10.6. Remember:

1   Find out as much as you can about your team before you take action.
2   Think about how your own behaviour affects the situation.
3   Choose the time, place and your approach to follow-up talks carefully (see the section on 'Counselling' in the next chapter).

Case Study 10.6:   *For*
STRATEGIES FOR 'DIFFICULT' TEAM   *reflection*
MEMBERS

These diagrams, produced by the Careers and Counselling Unit at the University of Leeds, outline some possible strategies for dealing with team members who, for three different reasons, are not contributing to the team in a positive and effective way.

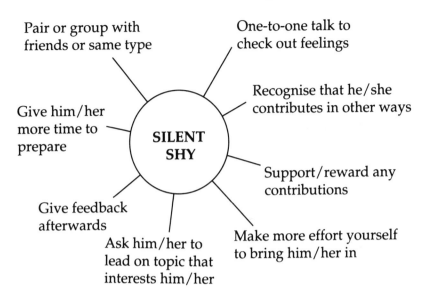

Pair or group with friends or same type

One-to-one talk to check out feelings

Give him/her more time to prepare

Recognise that he/she contributes in other ways

SILENT SHY

Support/reward any contributions

Give feedback afterwards

Ask him/her to lead on topic that interests him/her

Make more effort yourself to bring him/her in

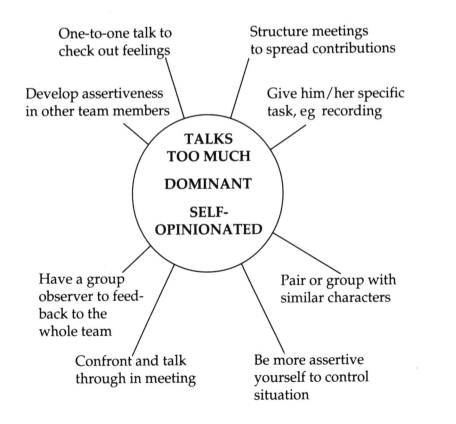

One-to-one talk to check out feelings

Structure meetings to spread contributions

Develop assertiveness in other team members

Give him/her specific task, eg recording

TALKS TOO MUCH

DOMINANT

SELF-OPINIONATED

Have a group observer to feedback to the whole team

Pair or group with similar characters

Confront and talk through in meeting

Be more assertive yourself to control situation

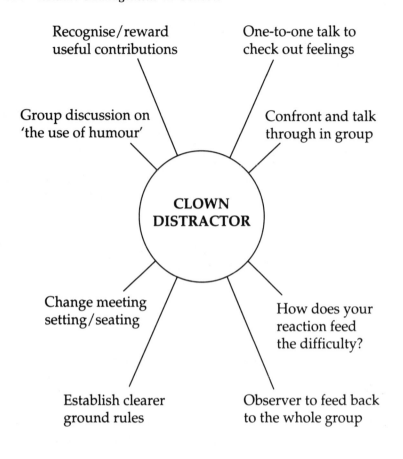

Recognise/reward useful contributions

One-to-one talk to check out feelings

Group discussion on 'the use of humour'

Confront and talk through in group

CLOWN DISTRACTOR

Change meeting setting/seating

How does your reaction feed the difficulty?

Establish clearer ground rules

Observer to feed back to the whole group

Delegation

The ability to delegate is one of the most important skills a manager can have. Delegation is vital to both you and the team, because:

- it helps to build the team
- it develops the skills and confidence of team members
- it allows the team to do a more effective job
- it allows you, as team leader, to retain your sanity!

Some middle managers (and indeed some senior managers) in schools still feel guilty about delegating – surely they are paid more to be head of department, or whatever, so they should be doing the whole job. This is a dangerous notion. Anyone who thinks like this is not thinking as a manager.

One definition of management is that it is *achieving objectives through others*. We would argue that this definition applies in schools as much as in any commercial organisation. As a middle manager you cannot hope to achieve all the objectives of your department on your own – indeed you should not even try. Your job as head of department, is to *manage* the operation of the department in such a way that its objectives are achieved. If you cannot do it all yourself, you have to delegate. **Successful delegation is a key to successful management.**

Ten pointers to successful delegation

1 Recognise that time spent on training someone to do a job is repaid many times over.
2 Delegate as much as you can – in this way you will leave yourself free to do the jobs *only you* can do.
3 Be ruthless with yourself, do not just delegate the jobs you do not like doing and keep the ones you enjoy – delegate on the basis that the job could and should be delegated.
4 Select the best person for the task, and make sure that person receives the training necessary to do the job.
5 Clearly define the task you are delegating, and make sure that the person who is carrying it out knows exactly what is expected of them.
6 Do not delegate exceptional tasks, such as
   • vital jobs that only you can/should do
   • tasks requiring confidentiality or particular sensitivity
   • new or ill-defined tasks that may prove difficult
7 Maintain a degree of control appropriate to the skill and experience of the person to whom you delegate – check progress to ensure that the job is being done
8 When you delegate a task, stress results rather than methods – you are delegating the responsibility of *doing* the job.
9 Use the opportunity of delegating to widen team members' experience and horizons – delegation is vital for staff development.
10 Real delegation requires judgement and faith in others – look to use these qualities whenever you delegate.

It is worth elaborating on Point 5 in the checklist above – *clearly define the task you are delegating, and make sure that the person who is carrying it out knows what is expected of them.* If you are asking someone to take on a task, it is only fair that you brief them properly – it will help the person do a better job, and it may save you time and trouble later on.

The Counselling and Career Development Unit of the University of Leeds has devised this list of questions as a checklist for briefing a delegate.

1   Responsibility
  • What is the precise task to be delegated?
  • What is its purpose?
  • What are its limitations (including time)?
  • How do the delegate's responsibilities tie in with other people's?
  • What are the criteria by which successful completion of the task will be judged?
2   Authority
  • How much freedom (including money and resources) does the delegate have to do the job?
  • To what extent will the delegate be able to control the activities of others?
  • In which areas will the delegate need to refer or share decision making, and to or with whom?
3   Accountability
  • To whom is the delegate accountable in this task?
  • What is expected of the delegate in terms of performance and standards?
  • For how long is the task delegated?
  • When and how often will the task be reviewed?
  • When and how often will there be an opportunity for feedback?
  • What procedures are required if mistakes occur?

Case Study 10.7:   *For action*
DELEGATION ISSUES

A

A note from Rob Willis to Simon Tucker, Head of the Science
Faculty:

> Dear Simon,
>
> I am writing to you about the draft profile you asked me to outline for lower school Integrated Science. I am simply not going to have time to do it for the meeting next week. Since I came out of hospital I have found things are rather on top of me, and I have not managed to complete my basic workload, let alone extra things. I must also confess that I am finding it rather difficult, and I think that it would be much better if you did the draft profile yourself.

Simon thinks that Rob is capable of the task. Rob agreed to take it
on, and agreed the time scale of a month for the work. Rob's
operation was on his ankle, and he was in hospital for three days.

How would you advise Simon to respond to this note?

B

Angela Bowles talking to Ian Murray after the Personal & Social
Education (PSE) team meeting:

'I enjoy teaching PSE a lot. I think it's a very valuable part of the curriculum, and I understand why it is so important to create PSE assignments which suit the needs of our pupils. In most cases the packaged products just don't work, whereas the children really enjoy the ones we have produced ourselves. I don't even mind the extra work involved because I like being part of a team which works creatively.

But what really irritates me is Margaret's approach. She is always nagging on about our being a team, and all having to pull our weight. Well, we do. There are a lot of assignments ready now, but what does she do herself, apart from grumble about all the hard work she has to do? I'd respect her a lot more if she gave a real lead by producing examples of good assignments, or tackling a really hard one herself, or helping me when I get stuck – like you do. All Margaret seems to do is nag us. When she goes on like that I get terribly irritated, so when she asks for volunteers to deal with a topic that actually interests me, I find myself thinking "she's the team leader, let her do it".'

1   *What would you consider to be the main mistakes Margaret is making in her role of team leader.*
2   *What has she not understood about the process of effective delegation?*

Case Study 10.8:   *For action*
RESTRUCTURING FACULTY RESPONSIBILITIES

Vivienne Michael, Head of the Social Science Faculty, has circulated this paper before a faculty meeting.

Bestwick Park School
Social Science Faculty

Delegation and Restructuring Responsibilities

1   Purpose of this paper

My recent pregnancy leave gave me the opportunity to do what

I hope has been some constructive thinking about how the faculty is organised and in this paper I shall make some proposals for restructuring, which I should like you to think about so that we can discuss them next week at the faculty meeting.

2   My reasons for making these proposals

Now that Mrs Gatlin is Head, the school itself is changing and I think the faculty needs to review how it operates.

When Mr Smith was Head, he delegated almost nothing, even to his deputies, and had very low expectations of his middle managers. As Head of Faculty I had no real idea of how the school was run and what was going on in it.

Mrs Gatlin takes a very different approach and expects her section heads to take a much greater part in running the school. She is generally more participative. Through the responsibilities she delegates, she is developing us by giving us the opportunity to undertake, shadow and discuss different tasks. This is good on-the-job training for me, and in turn the Head has told us that she expects her middle managers to give you similar opportunities within each faculty.

I like this whole approach and would like to introduce it into the Social Sciences Faculty.

3   General principles

a) The Heads of Department within the Faculty (Geography, Social Studies, Economics) will continue to have overall responsibility for their subject areas and the proposed reconstruction will in no way reduce their autonomy.

b) Tasks should be divided fairly. I have no wish to overburden anyone; we shall need to discuss as a group the principles on which we shall allocate responsibilities and what it is reasonable to expect of each person.

c) It is my job to see that you are clear about what you are responsible for and how you go about it. Some training may be needed before you take over a task that is new to you.

d) I shall be prepared at any stage to show you what to do, to rethink the task or to give general support and advice. (Please do not think that this means that I consider myself a paragon in any way!)

e) Once a task is delegated, I should leave you the freedom to carry it out and should not interfere unless there is good reason. Please do not think you have been abandoned, however, as it is always ok to discuss things with me.

f) The division of the tasks should be strategic. It would be improper for me simply to dispose of the more routine jobs and I should not dream of doing so. The idea is that everyone should gain experience of a variety of areas and get the chance to take decisions. It will, of course, include quite a lot of administration, because that is in the nature of running a department.

g) We shall need to decide how long a person should hold a particular responsibility. Too long in the job makes you stale and there is no challenge. Too short a time and you can't make your mark on it. The whole idea is to give each person a variety of experiences in a fairly structured yet democratic situation, so a regular rotation of responsibilities is an important aspect of the proposed faculty reorganisation.

h) You should also be given the opportunity to shadow areas that are not actually delegated. Here I suggest that you think about where your own interests lie and I shall try to accommodate you.

i) An important part of delegation is to provide each member of the faculty with some opportunity to take the chair at our meetings. As I do not think it appropriate to rotate the chair at every meeting, one of the things we shall need to discuss is possible ways to delegate chairing meetings or parts of meetings.

4   Possible methods

I have done some reading and thinking about how we should go about this and it may be helpful if I indicate the possibilities. There seem to be three main ways of going about dividing up responsibilities:

a) Each person could take responsibility for a year group or section of the syllabus. Although I am perfectly willing to do this if it is what you prefer, my own feeling is against a horizontal division of responsibilities because I do not think it gives sufficient width of experience. Although I do not consider lower school work is easier than upper school work, upper school tends to carry more status, so I do not want to limit anyone's career opportunities.

b) Responsibilities could be based on our aims as a faculty ie as expressed in our faculty document. This could prove an interesting and profitable exercise for us, but I think in practice it would be difficult to do and I do not want to overburden us. (It could be possible to use skills in a similar way to aims and this might be easier).

c) There could be a number of areas or aspects of responsibility. This would involve starting from my job description as head of department and dividing the tasks into three sections:

  i) Areas suitable for delegation.

  ii) Areas which should be managed by the department acting as a team.

  iii) Areas which should remain my personal responsibility and not be delegated at all.

Using my job description or listing the main tasks undertaken by the faculty as the basis for discussion of delegation seems to me the most viable method, but I did not want to preclude all discussion on this issue. Really these are suggestions aimed at getting us started – once we have decided the method we still have to give a lot of thought to how we allocate the responsibilities. I hope you will have time to give this paper some thought before you come to the meeting on Monday. You will probably have different and much better ideas than me and all ideas and suggestions will be very welcome.

Vivienne Michael.

Vivienne has produced a very structured paper that focuses the discussion onto how delegation could be implemented in the faculty, rather than on the issue of whether delegation should exist.

1 *What does the document indicate about Vivienne's management style?*

2 *What management skills is she employing? How successful might they be?*

3 *How do you think that different people within the faculty might react to this document?*

Chapter 11
Staff Development –
the Team

Of all those responsibilities for adults we undertake, that for their development as professionals is arguably the most important and the most difficult. The moment a teacher becomes a Head of Department, he or she has entered into the in-service training business. In fact one way to look at a department is to see it primarily as an in-service training enterprise. The importance of this part of the job is clear when we realise that without it all the other responsibilities that a Head of Department has for the curriculum will not flourish.

(Michael Marland, *Departmental Management*,

Heinemann, 1981)

What is staff development?

One of the aims of management is to make the best use of the skills and abilities of the people with whom they work. This is just as true for the middle managers as for the senior managers in a school or company. In order to make best use of human resources, to better achieve the aims of the organisation, people's skills and abilities need to be developed to their full potential. This is what staff development is all about.

As the quote from Michael Marland points out, staff development is something that must be the concern of Heads of Departments and team leaders; indeed this function is nowadays often identified as a 'key area' in a middle manager's job description. Marland's view is supported by one of the conclusions of the Welsh Office Research Project on Heads of Departments.

Whether you see your role primarily as a teacher or a manager, you will regard the professional development of your departmental staff (including yourself) as being of fundamental importance. As a teacher you will be concerned that every individual for whom you have responsibility – staff as well as pupils – is encouraged and supported in reaching his or her full potential. From a managerial standpoint, improvement in the range and quality of staff expertise is crucial to the department's most valuable resources and is an investment for the future well-being of the school. Professional development of staff not only results in increased effectiveness within the department, it also leads to enhanced job satisfaction amongst colleagues, and, in a period of reduced promotional opportunities, this is of paramount importance.

The two quotes above are stressing three very important points:

1 Staff development at department/team level is crucial to the effectiveness of the school as a whole.
2 Staff development is an essential concern of all middle managers who are team leaders.
3 The task of staff development is not an easy one for many middle managers to take on.

However good a teacher you may be yourself, it is not at all easy to take on the responsibility for the development of your fellow professionals. This is an area where, up until now, little or no training has been provided for middle managers in schools. Thus it is not surprising that it is an area of their jobs in which many middle managers lack confidence. The purpose of this chapter is to offer you some ideas on what you could be doing on staff development.

Some schools have a professional tutor or Deputy Head who has an overall responsibility for staff development and INSET. If this is the case in your school this is the person to whom you can go to seek advice and guidance. However, the presence of a professional tutor in the school does not mean that this person can, or should, do your staff development job for you – that is ultimately your responsibility.

Staff development can be considered from two standpoints: development of the team, and development of individuals within the team, although there is a clear overlap between the two.

Part of your job as a middle manager is to balance the staff development needs and demands of the individuals with what you consider are the best interests of the team as a whole. The question of releasing staff for out-of-school INSET courses is a classic case in which this balance needs to be achieved. There is no doubt that good courses can make a major contribution to the professional development of teachers, yet at times it seems as if this might be at the expense of actually teaching children, which is the prime aim of the school and the team. Similarly, with the introduction of local management in schools, it is increasingly common for departments to cover colleagues' planned absences from within the team's resources, so again the needs of the individual and the team need to be balanced.

This 'balancing act' is something that must be faced. To take the attitude that teaching children is the most important function of a teacher, so teachers should only be absent from the classroom in cases of illness or emergency, is akin to burying your head in the sand. Certainly too many absences can harm the relationship between a teacher and his or her class, but just as importantly, without the necessary professional development (in whatever form) a teacher runs the risk of stagnation, demotivation, and depressed morale.

One approach to finding this balance is to take a positive attitude. The development needs of the individual and of the team are not as incompatible as people sometimes claim. For one thing, staff development does not necessarily mean absence from the classroom. Furthermore, the development of individuals can be harnessed for the good of the team as a whole. Perhaps members of your team are ambitious for promotion, and in order to establish their credentials for promotion are prepared to make a considerable contribution to the work of the team – there is scope for staff development activities of mutual benefit in this situation which a good team leader can harness. Perhaps, as one of the outcomes of being released for out-of-school INSET, a member of the team might agree to undertake development work for the team linked to that INSET.

In the next chapter we consider staff development at the level of the individual. This chapter focuses on team development aspects of INSET and staffing policy, although we would repeat that individual and team development needs must often be viewed as two sides to the same coin.

INSET for the team

In-service training, or INSET, is now big business. INSET in various forms is provided by LEAs, by Higher Education institutions, by consultants, and within the school itself. School-focused INSET is an increasingly important part of the mix, particularly now that more of the budget is being devolved to school level.

INSET is often defined in a very narrow way – it is thought of in terms of 'courses' and 'Baker days'. These can make a significant contribution, but more important is the in-service training that can be going on in school as a continuing process, and it is in this aspect of INSET that the team leader has a crucial role to play.

Planning INSET

If INSET is going to form a major element in the staff development of your team, you will want to involve the team members in planning it – staff development has to be a shared process.

A good starting point for planning INSET might be to discuss the question

- What is INSET, and why do we need it?

The quotations about staff development and INSET on pages 172–173 might form a useful discussion stimulus. It is worth spending time on getting a good, shared understanding of the whole concept, because it will increase people's willingness to participate. Other discussion themes in the initial planning process might be:

- What INSET have team members had over the past year/two

years? What impact did it have on their work in school?
- What is 'good' INSET?
- How do we use INSET to meet the needs both of the team, and of the individuals within the team?

Once you have discussed the ideas behind staff development and INSET, and highlighted a number of views and priorities, you can turn your attention to planning your actual INSET activities. Some ideas are outlined in the next section. There are no hard and fast rules we can offer, as your planning will have to reflect your particular circumstances and priorities. However, it might be worth bearing four points in mind as you plan:

1 Avoid trying to do too much or spreading your net too widely. Establish your key priorities and focus your INSET programme on these priorities as far as possible.
2 Consider how you are going to spread INSET opportunities among the members of the team, taking into account the three needs – the task, the team, the individuals.
3 Consider how, once INSET has taken place, you are going to harness that experience to improve the work of the team.
4 Consider how you are going to evaluate the INSET, so that you can make the most effective use of precious INSET resources in the future.

Forms of INSET

1 *Meetings*
Your team meeting is an obvious vehicle for in-service training. The skills required to run effective meetings are discussed elsewhere in this book, and helping the members of your team to acquire these skills is part of your staff development role.

Team meetings can also be used in a number of other ways as INSET sessions. They can be used as seminars or workshops on specific educational issues relating to the work of the team and school. They can be used as planning sessions where, for example, a series of team meetings are used to develop a new scheme of work or assessment.

2 *Teaching collaboratively*
Teaching or working collaboratively with another member of the

team can be a very valuable form of INSET. Here are some suggestions as to how this can be done:

- Observation of each other's lessons. It is usually more effective to focus your observation on one or two particular aspects of the lesson – perhaps the pupil-teacher interaction, or the style of teacher questioning.
- Planning a topic/assignment, or developing teaching materials jointly. This could be followed by some team teaching of the topic, or joint evaluation of your own teaching of it.

3 *Visits to other schools or institutions*
This can be very valuable, particularly for colleagues who have spent a long time in their present school. How do other people set about doing things in their school? What good ideas do other people have for tackling this or that area of their work? What do we currently do that compares favourably with others' efforts?

Two notes of caution about visits as INSET. First, you need to choose the place you visit carefully. Seek advice, perhaps from an LEA adviser, or from middle manager colleagues in other schools. There is not much point in spending valuable INSET time and money going to see things from which you will not gain much – either because not much is happening in the place you visit, or because the other school is too different from yours for the experience to be readily transferable.

Second, when you arrange the visit, have a specific purpose in mind, and make sure that the school that has agreed to receive your visit is aware of your purpose. Structure your time on the visit in a way that helps you achieve that purpose. One approach that can help with this is to arrange for two members of your team to make the visit together – they will have the chance to talk through their impressions and experiences, and to analyse the outcome of the visit more thoroughly.

4 *Using external courses*
Selective use of external courses, whether run by the LEA or other provider institutions, can be very useful, but the opportunities for members of the team are likely to be limited. How do you choose who should go on a course?

You could, as team leader, go on all the courses yourself. This would be a mistake, as not only could it cause resentment, but it also prevents you from properly executing your role as a developer of your team. Your aim might well be to give everyone the chance to go on one or more courses during the year, basing your choice either on people's interests or needs, or by simply rotating opportunities. As long as it is clear that you are prepared to treat each member of the team fairly you do not have to stick rigidly to one system.

Two notes of caution about using external courses. First, your use of external INSET courses should be geared to meet the priorities of the team or of individuals within the team. It is all too easy to respond to course opportunities on an ad hoc basis, as notification of each course reaches you. Try to plan ahead over the year as a whole; find out what is on offer, and target your INSET time to meet what you have identified as your team priorities for the year.

Second, make the time people spend on external courses work for the team. You have the right to expect some end product from someone attending a course – at the very least a report back to the team as a whole. Ideally when someone attends a course the end product should be increased expertise or knowledge which benefits both that person, and the work of the team as a whole. Some schools or departments use standard course evaluation forms; this at least guarantees some feedback beyond the level of 'Lunch was OK' or 'Complete waste of time'. If the person judged the course to be a waste of time, as team leader you may wish to discuss the reasons with that person, and if appropriate raise the matter with whoever ran the course.

5   *School-based or team-focused INSET*

Increasingly INSET is viewed as an activity which is most effectively based in the school itself, either as a whole-school or a department/team activity. There are important advantages in this approach, and also some potential disadvantages. The major advantages are that you can involve everybody in the INSET programme, and gear the activity to meet particular needs you have identified as being an INSET priority.

One possible disadvantage is that there may not be anyone in the team or school with the expertise you need for a specific INSET activity. It may be possible to overcome this by bringing in people from outside, such as advisory teachers or advisers, or people from educational institutes.

Organising school-based INSET does put the onus for planning and execution on people within the school. Planning and costing INSET is now an important element in a middle manager's job. Proper planning is essential – if you expect colleagues to give up time to INSET you must ensure that it is well organised, and stimulating.

Case Study 11.1:   *Exemplar*
A DEPARTMENT'S ANNUAL INSET PLAN

Design Faculty INSET

Aims
The overall aims of INSET for the faculty are:

a) To improve and develop the work of the faculty
b) To develop the individuals within the faculty
c) To establish contacts with colleagues beyond the school

Priorities
The two main priorities for faculty INSET next year are:

a) More active teaching and learning strategies
b) Management training

Both these priorities match existing school priorities for INSET.

Methods
INSET will take the form of:

a) Attendance at County courses
b) Visits to other schools
c) Work within the faculty, with the help of the adviser

Objectives
The objectives of INSET link with two faculty objectives

a) To develop a modular design course for Lower School, for introduction the year after next. This will involve: developing more active teaching and learning approaches; curriculum development work on the new course.

b) To develop closer links between the departments in the faculty, and to further develop management techniques

Proposed INSET programme
Modular course

1	County course on 'Active Learning'	2 staff × 1 day	Oct
2	Visits to other schools	2 × 2 half days	Oct–Nov
3	Baker Day – report back on 1 & 2	All	Dec
4	County course on 'IT in CDT'	1 × 1 day	Jan
5	Curriculum development work in school with adviser	All × 2 half days	Feb–Mar

Management training

1	County course Follow up by HoDs	1 × 3 days	Feb

Costs
The maximum cost in supply days would be:

County courses and visits	9 days
In-school INSET	10 days

Case Study 11.2:   *For action*
AN ISSUE ARISING FROM EXTERNAL INSET

Mrs Gatlin, the Head, has passed this letter to Mr McTavish, the Head of Mathematics, with a request for information on Mr Jones's absence record asap. Mr Jones has recently returned to teaching after a break of some years, and is teaching a new A level syllabus as well as GCSE courses. He has had four days out of school on INSET courses, and there are two more days planned for later in the year.

Re: Victoria Carmichael   (4B)

Dear Mrs Gatlin,

I feel that I must write to you because yet again Victoria has missed her mathematics lesson because Mr. Jones has been out of school, apparently on a course. I know that a substitute teacher is always provided, but that person is not usually a trained Mathematician, and I am very concerned that Victoria has missed so many lessons in such a vital subject. Could you explain to me please what the school's policy is about teachers missing lessons to go on courses, as this did not occur so frequently when my older children were at the school.

Yours sincerely
Ruth Carmichael.
RUTH CARMICHAEL   (MRS)

1   *If you were in Mr McTavish's place, how should you respond to this particular problem?*

2   *As a Head of Department how can you reconcile the loss of pupil contact time with the needs of staff development/INSET, particularly in view of the fact that many departments are having to react to a number of externally-imposed changes?*

Case Study 11.3:   *For action*

A WHOLE-SCHOOL INSET ISSUE

All the Heads of Department at Bestwick Park School have received this memo from Mrs Gatlin, the Head:

The lack of a clear marking policy in schools is regularly criticised in HMI reports, and there is a strong recommendation that all schools should have such a policy.

I can find no indication that Bestwick Park has a marking policy, and I think that it is urgent that we, as a school, address ourselves to this issue. My feeling is that the best place to start is with individual departments.

I should like each department, as a piece of departmental INSET, to devote its next department meeting to examining its present practice, making proposals for its marking policy, and encapsulating its conclusions in a short working paper to be submitted to me before half-term.

I shall then use a Head of Department Meeting to consider these papers, using them as a basis from which to develop a whole school policy. This policy will be discussed and finalised at a full staff meeting.

1   *Comment on Mrs Gatlin's approach to developing a whole-school policy.*
2   *What strategy would you use to respond to this request from the Head?*

Staffing policy

Your staffing policy is the way you decide how you allocate particular classes to the members of your team, yourself included. In terms of staff development this policy can have a major impact on the breadth of a teacher's experience, and on the way a teacher is in a position to contribute to the overall work of the department.

Once again your staffing policy will need to take account of the three needs – the team, the task and the individuals. Look at the following examples:

Andrew has asked you if he can teach Sixth Form A level work, which he has not done before. He needs the experience in terms of his own career development, but your decision must also take into account: i) Andrew's ability to do the job – will he be an effective A level teacher? ii) How will giving him A level teaching affect the rest of the team?

You may want to ask Mary to be Lower School Co-ordinator. To do the job well she ought to teach many more lower school classes

*than she does now, but this will mean that she can no longer have
a Sixth Form group. What would Mary prefer, and what is best
for her development? What is best for the work of the team?*

Decisions on staffing must be yours, although you have to
justify your decisions to senior management. In establishing a
staffing policy you could consider these points:

1 The policy should be as fair as possible – the head of
   department should not be seen to teach a privileged timetable!
2 People should normally have as wide a spread across the years
   and abilities as possible. It may not be possible each year, but
   can be organised over a period of years if necessary. This is
   important not only to widen team members' experience, but
   also to prevent a situation where over-specialisation makes
   timetabling more difficult.
3 The process of determining staffing should include discussions
   with people to find out what they would like to be doing, and
   what it is agreed they need to be doing. In the end you may
   not be able to accommodate people's wishes – the final decision
   must be yours.

Case study 11.4 shows the situation facing a Head of Geography
as regards allocating staff to teaching groups next year.

Case Study 11.4:   *For action*
STAFFING EXERCISE

The school is a mixed 11–18 comprehensive. Situated in the
suburban part of a large town, the school draws extensively from
low cost housing estates. 40% of pupils come from middle class or
'aspiring' working class homes. 15% of pupils are from ethnic
minority groups, mainly Asians, including some recent immi-
grants. The number on the school roll is falling slowly.

Geography is taught as a separate subject throughout the school.
All lower school Geography is taught in mixed ability classes.
GCSE sets in the 4th and 5th years are divided into X (upper) and
Y (lower) bands.

Current staffing

The details below outline the current staffing position in the department, and how staff are allocated to teaching groups.

Staff information

Staff	Age	ppw	Other info	Qualifications
Cathy James 34 (Head of Dept)		32	Second year in the school	Graduate, BA Geog
Robin Davies 41 (2nd in Dept)		36	Leaving at the end of year	Certificate
Richard Willis 23 (Probationer)		20	10 ppw History 4 ppw PE	BEd
Brenda Evans 52 (Late entrant)		35	i/c internal examinations	Graduate, BSC Geol

Staffing needed					*Staffing available*	
Year	1	7 groups × 3 periods =	21	CJ	32
	2	7 × 3	= 21		
	3	7 × 3	= 21	RD	36
	4	5 × 4	= 20	RW	20
	5	6 × 4	= 24		
				BE	35
	6	1 × 4 GCSE			
		1 × 6 A level	= 10	TOTAL	123
	7	1 × 6	= 6		
		TOTAL	123		

Staffing used

	Yr 1	2	3	4	5	6	7		Total
CJ	—	3	3	8	12	3	3	=	32
RD	3	6	9	4	4	7	3	=	36
RW	9	3	—	4	4	—	—	=	20
BE	9	9	9	4	4	—	—	=	35
	21	21	21	20	24	20	6		123

Staffing for next year

Cathy James, as Head of Department, will have to make a number of changes in her staffing for next year. The situation is as follows:

- The school roll is falling – next year will be only 6 form entry and geography will have only 10 groups in the 4th and 5th years.
- Robin Davies, the 2nd in the department, is leaving to take up a pastoral post – the Head is not able to replace him with another full-time Geographer.
- Richard Willis is still needed to teach 10 periods of History and 4 periods of PE, but he will lose the 2 free period 'probationer allowance' he had last year.
- Cathy James and Brenda Evans will have the same free period allowance.
- To make up the shortfall Cathy is facing in Geography staffing (with the departure and non-replacement of Robin), the Head is offering two people, each of whom could teach up to a maximum of 10 periods of Geography a week.

    Janet Roberts – Deputy Head
    Miss Roberts trained 25 years ago, with Geography as her main subject, but she has not taught the subject for some time.

    Paul Parker
    Paul is a member of the PE department, who has just completed his probationary year at the school; he has A level Geography, and Geography was a subsidiary subject for him at college.

In relation to both staffing policy and staff development possibilities:

1 *Analyse the HoD's staffing pattern in the current year.*
2 *Look at the information about the situation for the next year, and using tables like the ones for the current year:*
    a) Establish the staffing need for Geography next year.
    b) Establish what staffing is available for Geography.
    c) Suggest how Cathy James should use the allocated staffing – to balance the needs of task, team and individual.

Chapter 12
Staff Development –
Individuals

When I arrived at the school for my first year in teaching, the Head of Department gave me my timetable and a syllabus, showed me my classroom and the stock cupboard, and left me to get on with it. In that first year neither the Head, nor one of the deputies, nor my Head of Department even so much as put their nose round the door of my room. As it happens I was OK, and things went quite well. Later I asked one of the deputies how they knew I was alright, and he said 'It was always fairly quiet every time I walked past your room, so I knew that there couldn't be serious problems'.

(A teacher who qualified in 1977)

Your team will be made up of individuals who are at different stages of their careers, and who have different professional needs and aspirations. As team leader part of your responsibility is to provide some of the professional development they will need to reach their full potential.

One thing you will have to do is handle the induction of staff new to the school or to your team. You will certainly want to take a rather more professional approach than the senior colleagues of the teacher quoted above. Induction is not just for probationers, and so it is important to tailor induction programmes to the needs of colleagues who have moved from other schools, who are returning to the profession after a career break, or who are taking on new responsibilities within the school.

As we outlined in the previous chapter, staff development is also about providing professional support and stimulation for existing members of your team. We work in a rapidly changing educational environment, and at times we all need help in adapting to new roles or approaches. One of the most difficult tasks facing a manager can be to guide the professional development of a team member who is resistant to change, or who finds it difficult to accept or act on advice.

Case Study 12.1:
HELPING JESSICA

For action

Jessica Cram has recently joined the Biology department at Bestwick Park. She has two years' experience of teaching, and was delighted to gain the post as she had to move to the area for family reasons.

Jessica is rather intense and introverted, and is very anxious to meet the academic demands of the school, which has a high reputation in the area. Her previous school was not fully comprehensive, as it had few pupils who gained high grades at GCSE. Jessica did not have the opportunity to teach A level at her previous school.

She finds it difficult to communicate with other members of the Science department, although they are anxious to be friendly and helpful. They say that Jessica does sometimes ask for advice, but then she doesn't seem to make any use of their suggestions.

Just after half-term (in Jessica's first term) the Head received this note from a parent of a Fourth Year pupil:

I am becoming very concerned about the amount of Biology homework my daughter is receiving. The homework in this subject this term has regularly been very heavy indeed. Surely, even for GCSE, it should not be necessary for her to work for six hours, as she did last night just for her Biology homework?

The Head asks Christopher Jones, Head of Biology, to look into the matter. The pupil is taught by Jessica Cram.

1   *If you were Christopher Jones how would you handle this matter?*
2   *How would you set about trying to help Jessica?*

Induction

Induction is the introduction of someone into a new post; it is the process whereby someone new to a job is helped in getting to know the ropes and acclimatising to the school ethos – who's who in the school, how things operate, what is expected, and so on.

The quote at the start of the chapter indicated that the particular school concerned had a 'sink or swim' approach to new staff. Such a policy is increasingly rare nowadays, although it is probably true to say that induction can still be a rather haphazard process in many schools. Not having a properly thought-out induction process means that you are under-using a valuable resource. Any new job involves a learning period, during which the new person is operating at less than full effectiveness, but a good induction programme can substantially reduce this learning time. A good induction programme will also help a new person feel welcome, and accepted as part of the team.

Ten induction points to consider

1   Is there someone in the school with a responsibility to coordinate the induction of all new colleagues and post-holders?
2   Is there an LEA induction programme for teachers new to the authority?
3   What arrangements should you make for new colleagues after their appointment but before they take up post?
4   What arrangements should you make for new colleagues in their first week in post?
5   What arrangements can you make within your team to help new colleagues settle into their post, and the school?
6   How do you help new team members in curriculum matters?

7 How do you help new team members with any discipline/pastoral problems?

8 How can you help new team members with any personal difficulties, such as finding accommodation?

9 How can you set up a monitoring procedure that is sensitive to the needs and concerns of a new team member?

10 How can you set up a procedure, jointly with your new colleague, for regularly reviewing work and how he/she is settling into the school?

Before term starts

Some time after the interview, but before the appointee takes up post, is a good time to invite her or him to visit the school again. In most cases this visit is best organised by the Head of the main department in which the new colleague will be working. A visit is not always possible, but if it can be arranged it provides the new colleague with the opportunity to:

- meet her/his colleagues, including pastoral team leaders and the heads of other departments with whom she/he will be working;
- talk to the person who is leaving the post;
- obtain copies of the relevant school documents, such as the staff handbook, which will give an idea of how the school is organised;
- see and discuss teaching syllabuses;
- receive a personal timetable, if it is available;
- discuss the job description;
- look around the department rooms, and see the resources available;
- take away some textbooks and resources so that she/he can make a start on preparing some lessons.

If there is time it can be very useful for a new colleague to visit classrooms where lessons are in progress, and to be involved in a team meeting or planning session.

At the beginning of term

A useful first step is to go through the new colleague's timetable with them, as getting this sorted out will be one of their priorities.

Check whether there are (or are likely to be) any personal difficulties, such as accommodation or transport to and from school.

Ideally someone in the team should act as a guide and mentor to a new colleague for the first few weeks; this need not be the team leader, indeed, it is often better if the mentor is someone who is in a roughly similar position in the organisation.

Be careful not to overload a new colleague with briefing sessions in the first few days, or even weeks. Their overwhelming priority is likely to be to find their feet in the basics, so leave briefings to an appropriate time later in the first term if you can.

Induction for probationers

We have been referring to 'probationers' in this chapter, although it is not clear whether this term will continue in use for much longer, as one of the provisions of the 1988 Act is to replace the traditional one year probationary period with a two year introductory period. Whatever the precise legal status of teachers entering their first permanent post in schools, the general points made about induction in this section are likely to apply.

Most schools have arrangements for probationers. It is usual that they are given a slightly lighter timetable for the first year; one reason for this is to build in some time for on-the-job training. Many schools have a member of staff, sometimes called a 'professional tutor', who has responsibility for probationers, who arranges school-based INSET sessions and who is available to deal with any problems that arise. As a leader of a team which includes a probationer, you will need to liaise with the professional tutor, if your school has one. There may also be an adviser who has a role to play in supporting the probationer, with whom you will also want to liaise.

Whatever other support is available to a probationer it is still likely that the most important guidance and support will come from within the team, or teams, in which that probationer works. Thus the team leader has the most important role in the induction process. The areas in which a probationer may need some support include:

- preparing and structuring of lessons

- teaching at an appropriate level to stretch all pupils
- teaching mixed ability classes
- classroom organisation and management
- relationships with pupils, and discipline problems with either individuals or groups
- coping with the pressure of work
- following school/department marking and assessment policies

Schools use a variety of support strategies to help new colleagues.

1 *Joint planning work* – giving the probationer the chance to work with the team leader, or someone else from the team, on planning and developing teaching ideas and resources.

2 *Observing other people's lessons* – inviting the probationer to spend time in the lessons you or other experienced team members are teaching. This can be particularly useful if someone is having difficulty with a particular syllabus or age range.

3 *Using role play* – spending time with the probationer working through classroom situations which are proving difficult to handle, such as with disruptive pupils, or mixed-ability classes.

4 *Regular informal discussion sessions* – spending time, in a relaxed setting, talking about teaching approaches or about any concerns the probationer may wish to raise.

5 *Reviewing progress* – a somewhat more formal session to review progress can be useful, and might take place once every half term. Part of the review process might involve helping the probationer to identify particular aspects of their practice on which they could focus for the next half term.

Assessing probationers

The school has to make an evaluation of the quality of a probationer's work. One key aspect of this evaluation must be observation of the teacher at work with pupils, usually in the classroom. Observation is necessary, not only for assessment purposes, but also because it helps identify aspects of the probationer's work that might require the school to give more guidance and support.

As team leader you will play the most important role in the

observation and overall assessment process, although it is usual that others will also observe some of the probationer's work – a deputy, the Head, and often an LEA adviser. Having one's lessons observed can be a daunting and potentially threatening situation, particularly if there is not a tradition of 'open' classrooms in the school. When undertaking classroom observation these are some of the points you will want to consider:

1   *Clarify the purpose of the observation*

Discuss the purpose of the proposed observation with your probationer colleague, so that he/she is clear about its purpose. Is it simply an informal observation which the two of you will use as the basis of staff development discussions? Is it a more formal observation session which will form part of the school's probationer assessment process?

2   *Give plenty of notice*

Give your colleague plenty of notice, particularly if it is one of the earlier observation sessions. Once you have agreed the time and date of the session make this a priority action for yourself; cancelling the session at the last moment gives all the wrong messages about the importance you attach to the exercise.

3   *Discuss and agree the timing of observation sessions*

You may have clear views about when probationers should be observed during their first term and year, but also seek the views of the probationer. Some probationers may prefer to have time to come to grips with things before they are observed, others might welcome a classroom visit quite early on in the first term. There is no right or wrong approach, but we would suggest that towards the end of the first half-term is often about the right time for a first more formal observation session.

4   *Give the probationer some choice of groups to be observed*

In order to lessen any threat inherent in classroom observation, it can be a good idea to give your colleague a choice of which class is to be observed in the first instance; having someone observe work with a group with which they are more confident can make that first observation session a much more positive experience. You will want to observe lessons with contrasting groups at a later stage however, and so the observation schedule over the year is something you could discuss with the probationer at this early stage.

5 *Outline how you will operate during the observation session*
Discuss with the probationer the best way for you to operate in his/her classroom. Will you just be sitting somewhere at the back, passively observing? Would it be more appropriate for you to be more active and join in for parts of the lesson? Your approach will need to depend partly on the nature of the lesson that is planned.

6 *Make the time you spend observing effective*
To make a realistic assessment you will want to spend a reasonable amount of time in your colleague's classroom. Ideally you should be there for the full lesson, and certainly you will want to avoid the quick ten minute 'pop in' approach, which is both disruptive and ineffective.

In order to make a proper assessment of the quality of the lesson you may find it useful to use a structured observation schedule. Not only does a schedule help you to focus on a range of aspects of the lesson, it is also a very valuable tool for the feedback you will give afterwards. One example of an observation schedule is given in Case study 12.2.

7 *Give feedback after the observation session*
This is a crucial part of the whole process, and one which requires enough time. It may be that immediately after the lesson is not the best time for giving feedback, as one or both of you may be rushing off to another activity. Discuss the best time for feedback before you observe the lesson; if enough time is not available immediately afterwards, give some brief comments, preferably about the positive things you saw, and do the full feedback later, in more relaxed circumstances. If you can, try and arrange for the full feedback session to be on the same day, and certainly no later than the day afterwards.

It is usual practice for the school to write an assessment report on probationers at the end of the first term, and then again at the end of the first year. Although the report may actually be written by a senior manager, as team leader you will be closely involved. Make sure that your probationer colleague is fully aware of how the reporting process will operate. Case study 12.3 outlines some possible headings for a report.

In some schools this is an 'open' report, which the probationer can see and discuss. Whether or not the probationer has the opportunity to read the actual report, it is important that he/she has the chance to discuss what is said in it; this may be the responsibility of a senior manager, but if so, as team leader, you will also want to talk through the report with your colleague – sharing and discussion is a vital element of effective staff development.

Case Study 12.2:   *Exemplar*
A CLASSROOM OBSERVATION SCHEDULE

PROMPTS	COMMENTS

Start of the lesson
- Did the lesson start on time?
- Was the teacher aware of the 'mood' of the pupils?
- Did the pupils settle down to work mode quickly?
- Was the aim of the lesson clearly understood by all pupils?

Pupil activity
- Did pupils have a sound understanding of what they were being asked to do?
- Were the lesson activities well planned and prepared?
- Were the appropriate resources available for the planned activities?
- Were the activities differentiated appropriately to meet the needs of all pupils in the class?
- Did the lesson have pace, variety and challenge for all pupils?
- Did the activities allow pupils to

take some responsibility for their
own learning?

Classroom interaction
- Was the classroom atmosphere
  orderly and work-centred?
- Were any disruptions or behaviour
  difficulties handled effectively by
  the teacher?
- Was the interaction between
  teacher and pupils (as a whole
  class, in groups, with individuals)
  effective in promoting learning
  and understanding?
- Was the interaction among pupils
  positive and co-operative?
- Were all pupils encouraged to
  contribute to class or group
  discussion?

Teacher activity
- Was the teacher effective in
  motivating all the pupils?
- Did the teacher communicate
  effectively?
- Did the teacher respond well to
  the needs of individuals and
  groups?
- Did the teacher devote a
  proportional amount of time to
  girls and boys?

The end of the lesson
- Were the activities managed well
  to suit the time available?
- Was the lesson summarised in an
  appropriate manner?
- Did the pupils leave the room in
  an orderly way?

Case Study 12.3:
PROBATIONER REPORTS – SOME QUESTION HEADINGS

For reflection

This list is not intended to be either exhaustive, or prescriptive – the questions are suggestions for points you may wish to consider when assessing the progress and contribution of a probationer.

- What is the age and ability range of pupils taught?
- Are lessons usually well planned for the needs of the different classes taught?
- Are the resources used well chosen to meet the needs of pupils and classes of varying ages and abilities?

- Does he/she have a sound grasp of the subjects being taught?
- Is he/she able to stimulate and maintain pupils' interest in the subjects?

- To what extent has she/he attempted to get to know all the pupils as individuals? How far has she/he succeeded?
- Are pupils of all ages and abilities suitably extended and stimulated?
- Is the atmosphere in all classes one in which quality work and effort are valued?

- What resources and visual aids are being used, and to what effect?
- Is the use of language at an appropriate level for pupils and classes of varying ages and abilities?
- Is an appropriate range of approaches to teaching and learning used to good effect?

- Is classroom organisation effective?
- Do lessons start and finish to time?
- Is the teaching area kept in good order?

- Is the homework policy of the department/school being followed?
- Is pupils' work being marked according to school/department policy?
- Is a proper record being kept of (a) what is taught (b) the progress of individuals?

- Are relationships with pupils appropriate, and classroom

control satisfactory?

- Has he/she integrated into the department? Is he/she sensitive to the departmental ethos?
- Are relationships with other staff good? Is he/she sensitive to the ethos of the school?

- How has she/he contributed to the overall work of the department?
- How has she/he contributed to extra-curricular activities?

- Is he/she willing to accept advice and positive criticism?
- Has this report been discussed with the probationer?

Case Study 12.4: *For action*
A FAILING PROBATIONER

Meena Dawada is a probationer in the Geography department. This report on her was written by the Head of Department.

This is Miss Dawada's third term in the school, and things have gone from bad to worse. I strongly urge, if it is at all possible, that she reconsider her choice of career. Although she is conscientious, she does not seem to be able to build on advice or constructive criticism, and indeed seems to take every remark personally.

This is reflected in the classroom, where her lessons have seen one confrontation after another. Initially the problem was with her accent and the way she pronounces some words; our pupils, who themselves come from a variety of ethnic backgrounds, have found it very difficult to understand her. When pupils pick on this as a way of testing her classroom control, she becomes shrill and shouts at them, and a confrontation develops.

Various members of the faculty have demonstrated lessons for her. I have had her in my own lessons on many occasions, and we have had regular discussions on teaching methods, classroom control, and establishing good pupil-teacher relationships. But we do not seem to be able to make any progress, and this week there was an incident in a second year lesson, in which personal remarks were exchanged and half the class actually walked out of the lesson in support of a fellow pupil. This incident has been dealt with, but I must question Miss Dawada's future in teaching. She herself is insistent that she wants to continue teaching and pass her probation.

1 *Comment on this as a probationer report, and on the way the HoD has described and defined the problem.*
2 *Analyse the wider underlying management issues in this situation.*
3 *What action would you suggest the HoD take, in the short term and in the longer term?*

Induction for experienced teachers

While schools and LEAs commonly have induction programmes for probationers, it is not so common for experienced teachers. Induction for experienced teachers does not have to be an elaborate and time-consuming process, but to have a planned process for 'showing them the ropes' can pay dividends in helping a colleague over any initial teething troubles.

Good induction involves more than just a guided tour of the premises and a chat about the philosophy of the school. The aim of induction is to help a new colleague to become effective in his or her work as quickly as possible. The process, therefore, includes:

- letting your new colleagues know that guidance is available, and from whom;
- making sure that a new colleague is confident about what he or she should be doing, both in terms of the school's expectations of the post and the school/department priorities;
- arranging a number of informal opportunities to discuss progress, difficulties or uncertainties.

Case Study 12.5:   *For action*
ROLE UNCERTAINTY

Jean Stringer has recently joined the staff, to teach RE. Jean is an experienced teacher, returning to the profession after a break of some years. She is very conscientious about her work. In a conversation with the Head of RE she says that while she is enjoying the subject teaching very much, and things are going well, she is very uncertain about her role as a Fourth Year tutor. She says that she does not really know what she is meant to be doing during the weekly tutor period. She knows that there is supposed to be a programme of activities, but that the programme is rather confusing. Some of the activities that her Head of Year outlines in team briefing meetings seem to bear little or no relation to the school's published outline. In some weeks some material is put in her pigeon hole, but in other weeks she seems to have to produce her own activities. When she asked her Head of Year about all this, his response was 'Don't worry, we are all rather feeling our way at the moment. Use the materials if you want to, but if you would rather use your own ideas, then that's fine'.

1 *As Jean's Head of Department, what advice would you give her?*
2 *What wider actions should you take in this situation?*

Staff development and appraisal

The process of appraisal is an integral element in the effective professional development of staff, and yet the concept of appraisal is one that is often misunderstood. People's quite understandable concerns about appraisal often stem from the perception that it is some form of external assessment of their performance as a teacher. Because the aim of appraisal has not been made clear it is seen as potentially threatening.

What is the purpose of appraisal?

The only purpose of the sort of appraisal we discuss below is to help teachers to develop and enhance their professional skills. In simple terms it involves a constructive discussion between two people, usually the team leader and a team member, with the aim of working together on ways in which the work of the team can be improved.

This sort of appraisal is not about making one-sided judgements about the quality of a teacher's work. What it *is* about is having a proper and planned process for helping a teacher to develop his or her professional skills. It is thus a process of formative appraisal.

People who have been involved with this sort of formative appraisal, both in education and industry, are usually very positive about the benefits it can bring. We strongly believe that appraisal is a benefit, which for far too long has been denied to many teachers. Every teacher should have the right to a regular job review which helps them to identify what they are doing well, and which helps to identify areas of their work which need further development and support.

What are the advantages of appraisal?

A well thought out and well managed system of appraisal can bring substantial benefits to both individual team members and the team as a whole.

Individual team members
A good appraisal system:

- offers each individual an opportunity to share in discussion of team aims, tasks and priorities
- clarifies for each individual how her/his job fits in with the overall team task
- provides an opportunity for a review of priorities and performance
- helps in identification, and recognition, of strengths and areas of success
- helps in identification of areas of weakness and provides practical help in overcoming them
- identifies training needs and how they can best be met
- provides the opportunity for individuals to discuss career development
- enhances the individual's job satisfaction

The team as a whole
Appraisal:

- helps to develop a shared understanding of the team aims, tasks and priorities
- clarifies how individuals' jobs fit in with the overall team task
- reviews team priorities and performance
- provides opportunity to modify team organisation to meet changing needs and priorities
- improves communication and interchange of ideas within the team
- helps to identify potential within the team and encourages its development
- helps to motivate team members and enhance team performance
- identifies team training needs and how they can best be met

- helps to build the team into a more coherent unit, and to enhance the job satisfaction of team members

We would not like to give the impression that appraisal is all plain sailing. While the concept is one that can bring major benefits to both individuals and teams, there are some important points which need to be considered in order to make any appraisal system effective. *Time* is always one of the difficulties we face in schools, and appraisal does take time. Colleagues' perceptions can be another potential stumbling block in the introduction and operation of appraisal. Both these points, and many others, are considered in the sections that follow. We would like to emphasise that there is no one 'correct' system of appraisal, and a school or team needs to adapt and develop a system that meets its particular needs.

What sort of appraisal system?

A range of different approaches to appraisal are currently in use in both schools and industry. In this section there is not enough space to review them all, but you may want to research some of them in more detail; a number of LEAs have been running pilot schemes, and plenty of schools have set up appraisal systems, and you may find it useful to review the approaches they have tried.

The common feature of most school appraisal systems is that they involve two main elements – classroom observation and the appraisal 'interview'. The term interview is commonly used, although it perhaps gives a somewhat misleading impression; the appraisal interview is usually a structured but informal discussion session between two professionals.

The following criteria have been suggested for an effective appraisal system:

1 The people involved . . .
   - want it
   - understand it
   - are committed to it
   - are trained to participate in it
   - keep it under review and develop it
   - own it
2 The paperwork involved . . .
   - is simple and not too time-consuming

- is realistic and job related
- is open – in the sense that everyone knows what is involved
- is confidential between the appraiser and appraisee

3 The appraisal system is used for . . .
- the self-development of the individuals involved
- counselling on people's needs
- analysing people's training needs
- helping with people's career development

Introducing appraisal

Appraisal is still a controversial and sensitive issue, and so its introduction needs careful handling. For a team leader the easiest approach is to introduce appraisal as part of a whole-school scheme. However, this option may not be open to you. It is certainly harder to operate in isolation, but this is not necessarily a reason for not developing appraisal.

Assuming that you are considering appraisal which does not form part of a school system, how should you go about it? First, discuss your intention with the Head before you start any work with your team. Make sure that your development work really does involve all the members of your team, and avoid any perceptions that the system is being imposed. Make sure that you allow plenty of time and opportunity for the team to be involved in the development work – Murphy's Laws are particularly pertinent in the case of introducing appraisal!

> Nothing is as simple as it seems
> Everything takes longer than you think
> If anything can go wrong it will

Here are two INSET ideas which you could use at the start of the appraisal development process.

Brainstorming advantages and disadvantages

1 Divide a board or flipchart into two columns, headed TEACHER GAINS and TEACHER CONCERNS.
2 Outline the purpose of the session as an attempt to identify what any group of teachers (not just your team) might feel about the elements of appraisal which fall under these two headings.
3 To start with, accept all suggestions without discussion – just

note all the points made.

4 When the suggestions begin to dry up, ask the team to say which of the elements in each list they think are the most significant. The elements that are identified as significant can then form the basis of further discussion – why are they significant?

This sort of approach allows people to air their worries and concerns without making the exercise too personal. It also gives you, and the team, a good idea of the things you will need to bear in mind when developing your appraisal system.

Sharing experience
Appraisal operates in a number of schools and teams already. It can be very useful to invite colleagues, either from within your school or from another school, to share their experience with you. This gives your team the chance to ask the nitty-gritty 'What is it really like?' questions. To avoid the possibility of this sort of session becoming too negative it can be useful to structure it in a similar way to the exercise described above – first discussing 'gains' and then looking at 'concerns', and trying to focus on successes and solutions rather than on failures.

If there are no colleagues in school already involved in appraisal who you could invite to share their experience, you could ask your subject or school adviser to suggest a suitable person.

There is no getting away from the fact that some colleagues may have genuine concerns about appraisal, and so it is worth taking every appropriate opportunity to stress the following points.

- Appraisal is designed as a positive process – teachers have a right to appraisal as part of their professional development.
- The purpose of appraisal is developmental – not judgemental.
- Appraisal is used in industry and other professions – teaching is not the odd one out.
- The appraisal system is not set in tablets of stone – it can be modified and evolve to meet the needs of the team.
- The appraisal process is open and participative – a two-way exchange of ideas.
- The results of appraisal are confidential – what is said is not shared with anyone without agreement.
- Appraisal is an integral part of the job – it is not just an informal or irregular discussion that does not get followed up.

- Appraisal is not just for team members – the team leader will also be appraised.

There may be situations where, even after full discussions, one or more team members are fundamentally unhappy with the concept of appraisal. This is a difficult issue to handle, particularly if you are tackling appraisal in isolation and not as part of a whole-school process. If you are operating on a team basis only, it may be wiser to take a low-key approach with people who remain unconvinced, but to continue to involve everybody in the process of developing, reviewing and adapting the appraisal process. The benefits of appraisal stem largely from its ownership by the members of the team; to impose it on a colleague is likely to be counterproductive.

The sections which follow consider the two main elements of an appraisal system – classroom observation and the appraisal interview.

Classroom observation

A recent survey among deputy heads and senior teachers in an education authority revealed that systematic classroom observation was not part of the professional experience of senior managers. Very few claimed experience in pre-planning of classroom observation or in follow-up activity. Most had limited or no experience of regularly observing colleagues, or of being observed themselves; for most their only experience in observation was in the assessment of probationers. Nor did the majority think that recent changes in INSET arrangements were leading to any radical increase in this kind of activity.

We would not be surprised if a similar survey of Heads of Department and Year Heads produced very similar results. Yet as far back as 1971 Michael Marland was stressing the importance of classroom observation in the staff development work of the team leader.

It is perhaps surprising that very little has been written about classroom observation, except in the context of observing students or probationers. Although there are now quite a few books about appraisal on the market, they tend to have more to say about the appraisal interview than about observation. Yet we would argue that if teachers are not observed in the classroom, as part of the overall appraisal system, then appraisal loses much of its point.

How do you set about it?

A useful starting point might be to look back at the section on observing probationers, and then to consider what will be similar, and what will be different in the process of observing probationers and experienced colleagues.

The purpose is the same in both instances – to gain an insight into the colleague's classroom work, to approve good practice, and to provide guidance and help to the colleague to improve where necessary. The first obvious difference is that the probationer is a new teacher who will expect to be observed by someone in the school, and perhaps also by an outsider; observation is an accepted procedure for probationers, and your right to do it is unlikely to be questioned. Among the experienced colleagues in your team the situation could be very different if there is no tradition of classroom observation. Once someone has completed probation it is not impossible that, barring an HMI or LEA inspection, he or she will never be observed in the classroom again, undesirable as this situation might be. In some schools it is still unusual for one teacher even to enter the classroom in which a colleague is teaching. Thus the point is that, as team leader, you may need to negotiate your right to carry out classroom observation.

Another difference is that classroom observation as part of an appraisal process is going to be a regular cycle of observation, rather than the limited process undergone in the case of a probationer. Probationer observation usually has a general purpose – you observe all that happens from the bell at the start of the lesson to the bell at the end. The observation schedule you use will reflect this approach by covering a full range of classroom management and teaching and learning points.

This sort of general observation may be appropriate for the first one or two occasions you go into a colleague's classroom as part of the appraisal process, but after that it is likely that the observation will have a number of specific objectives which have been previously agreed between you and your colleague. Thus while you may be able initially to use a general observation schedule, like the one used for probationers, in due course you may need to design more specific schedules that reflect the observation objectives that the two of you have agreed.

The observation cycle

Classroom observation is part of the overall appraisal cycle, and you will need, as a team, to discuss and agree how and when the observation element will fit in. How you decide to time and structure the observation cycle is important.

Each observation exercise will have three stages – discussion beforehand, the observation itself, and the discussion afterwards. In this respect the points made about observing a probationer apply just as much to appraisal observation. Observation is a time-consuming process, particularly for you, if you are going to observe a number of lessons. In setting up the observation process the team could consider these points:

1 *When should the observation take place?* An obvious point is to avoid pressure points in a school year, or the very busy times in a colleague's week. Another consideration may be to leave the observation until a point in the year when colleagues feel that they have had the chance to settle in with their classes. Once an arrangement has been made to observe a lesson, this needs to be a priority commitment on your part; to cancel at the last moment gives all the wrong messages about the importance of the appraisal process.

2 *How many lessons should be observed?* This has to be a decision for you and your team, but you will want to avoid the 'just another burden' reaction. If the observation cycle is too demanding of time it will not be effective, and so it may be better to aim on the lower side initially; the reaction you want is 'that was good, why don't we do more of it?' You need to balance the time you have available with the need to observe enough – colleagues may not feel that it is fair to be appraised on the basis of observation that only involves an unrepresentative part of their teaching.

3 *Should the whole lesson be observed?* In an ideal world the answer is an emphatic yes, but your decision may be based on your time constraints. In discussions with your team you will want to establish agreement about the minimum length of observation time that is worthwhile.

4 *Which lessons should be observed?* To gain a rounded picture it will be useful to observe lessons with a range of age and ability groups; however, with time constraints it may only be possible to build up this rounded picture over time. In the initial stages of observation it may be best to suggest that each colleague selects the lessons for observation, as one of the objectives of the whole process is to approve colleagues' good practice. Later, when the observations may focus on more specific aspects, it would be possible to discuss the most appropriate lessons to visit.

5 *How should the pre-observation discussion be organised?* You will want to reach agreement on how far in advance this needs to be, what will be discussed, and what the colleague being observed needs to bring to the discussion by way of lesson outlines, etc. At this discussion you will want to agree on how you, as the observer, will operate in the lesson, which will depend to some extent on the type of lesson the teacher has planned.

6 *How should the post-observation discussion be organised?* The points made about probationer observation apply just as strongly here. The debriefing should be on the same day, and if possible, immediately after the lesson observed; again time constraints may operate, but the follow-up really should not be delayed longer than 24 hours. It is important that the discussion is not rushed, and is held somewhere private. This follow-up discussion is crucial to the whole process, and so your aim is to make it a positive experience. You could approach it as follows:

a) Identify and approve the good things you observed.
b) Give your colleague the chance to say how they felt the lesson went, and use this as a basis for further reinforcement of your colleague's strengths.
c) Invite your colleague to identify any aspects of the lesson that he or she felt did not go so well, or which could be improved.
d) Use your colleague's points as the basis for a discussion of approaches which might have been more effective, and if necessary introduce your own observations on possible points needing further development.

7　*Who should do the observation?* So far in this section the assumption has been that it will be the team leader who is going to be observing. Initially this is likely to be the case; once team confidence in the process has been established it may be that people feel that observation by their peers would be useful. In some teams some people are happy to have their lessons observed by a number of colleagues, or to have a lesson recorded on video, giving the opportunity for a subsequent whole team discussion.

A final point: do not forget yourself. If you are asking colleagues to allow their lessons to be observed by you, give them the chance to come in to some of your lessons as well.

The appraisal interview

The appraisal process is pulled together by an appraisal interview, which normally happens once a year. In some jobs the interview can occur at any time, but in schools it is usually done towards the end of the academic year.

The term 'interview', although most commonly used, is somewhat misleading – unlike a job interview, the appraisal interview is not about being questioned to see whether you are good enough. We stress again that the appraisal interview is about staff development, and its aim is to help each person to build up his or her professional expertise and to increase job satisfaction. The interview is a two-way exchange of views and ideas, which has at its end point the setting of goals and targets for the coming year.

Two documents are commonly used to aid the appraisal interview process – your colleague's job description, and a schedule which helps the person being appraised to review their work over the past year.

Training for appraisal interviews

An appraisal interview is not an easy task, for either party. It makes considerable demands on the sensitivity and people management skills of the appraiser. Ideally you should have training before you undertake appraisal interviews.

If your appraisal work is being carried out as part of a whole-school exercise, training will hopefully be available. If school-based training is not available you could:

- view one of the videos now available on appraisal interviewing (copies are likely to be available within the LEA);
- discuss and practise with a team leader colleague;
- discuss suitable INSET opportunities with your Head or adviser.

A common difficulty in such interviews is that the appraiser is too dominant. It is all-too-easy for the well-intentioned appraiser to end up offering advice and making suggestions left, right and centre, thus cutting out most of the contribution the appraisee could be making to the supposedly two-way process. For much of the time during an interview the good appraiser will be:

- listening attentively and responsively;
- asking the sort of questions which help to draw information and ideas from the person being appraised;
- being sensitive to the mood of the interview so that it can be made as positive as possible.

Appraisal interviews will be easier with some colleagues than with others. In some instances it may be your professional responsibility to discuss with someone things that they will not find easy to talk about, or perhaps even to admit. To do this in a way that is positive and not threatening will make very considerable demands on your skills as an appraisal interviewer. Being realistic you will not be able to develop the full range of appraisal skills without practice and experience. What you can do is evaluate rigorously your own performance as an interviewer after each appraisal interview you undertake – to identify what you need to improve, and set yourself targets for how you are going to do this.

Preparing for the interview

Both of you will need time to prepare for the interview. The person being appraised will need to think back over the past year. Experience suggests that this process is helped by asking people to fill in a short review schedule, such as the example included in

Case Study 12.8. The schedule usually invites the person being appraised to think about the positive and negative aspects of their work over the past 12 months. It is important that there is plenty of opportunity to be positive, as too negative a focus can have a significant impact both on the way the interview proceeds and on its outcome.

You will want to see the completed schedule in advance, as it will help you to identify what you would like to discuss at the interview. It will not be possible, or constructive, to discuss everything in depth at the interview, and it may be useful to set an agenda. The agenda might follow this outline:

1 Brief comments and discussion of points made in Review Schedule
2 Further discussion on three identified items:
   a) item identified by appraiser
   b) item identified by person being appraised
   c) item identified by mutual agreement
3 Discussion and agreement on goals and targets:
   a) agreement as to extent this year's goals have been achieved
   b) agreement on goals and targets for next year
   c) agreement on a possible programme of INSET/professional development for next year.

Conducting the interview

There is no set way of setting up and conducting an appraisal interview. The points made in Chapter 7 on running meetings will also apply here, as will many of the points in the section on counselling which follows later in this chapter.

Time and place are important. You need enough time, and a relaxed and private setting. Easy chairs and a cup of coffee are perhaps the ideal, and certainly the interview must never be conducted by the appraiser sitting behind a desk!

If you have agreed an agenda, use that to structure the discussions, though you may not wish to be bound by an agenda too rigidly. Whether or not you have an agenda, start from the positive, the successes and good experiences, and lead on to the more sensitive areas. Approve good work and achievements, clarify which areas of work require particular attention, discuss which difficulties could have been avoided; establish the areas of work in which your colleague would welcome your advice and support, and what form this support should take.

Appraisal is concerned with monitoring and assessing a colleague's professional performance and progress as a whole, but it is also concerned with helping your colleague to widen his or her professional horizons. It is a chance for the person being appraised to discuss career development and aspirations, and for the two of you to agree on the inservice programme appropriate for that person in the coming year and in the future.

Establishing goals and setting targets

By the end of the interview the two of you will want to have come to an agreement on an assessment of performance over the past year, in relation to your colleague's goals and targets. You will also have confirmed what your colleague's goals and targets should be over the coming year.

A goal is likely to relate to a broad area of a person's work, while a target will identify a more specific action which will help in the achievement of a goal. The goals and targets of one teacher are outlined in Case study 12.7 below.

The person's goals will form his or her action priorities for the coming year. Goals will not usually be completely new areas of work; it is not the intention to think of more things a person should be doing, but that a limited number of areas of existing work should form the focus for particular attention during the coming year.

The targets set will relate to the goals. Each target attempts to identify particular actions that need to be taken to help achieve the goals. Thus it is essential that targets are both realistic and attainable, and that they are described in terms that are clear and unambiguous. It may be possible to specify the timing, quantity, particular responsibility, means of evaluation etc in relation to a particular target – if so, it can be useful to do this in writing. This does not mean that the person does not have the right to use their own judgement about how to achieve the target, but only that you are providing a framework to help the person plan how they can achieve their agreed targets for the year.

How many goals and targets should be set? It is generally agreed that between four and six targets should be set. Two or more targets might link to the same overall goal, and so the number of goal areas may be less than the number of targets.

Fewer than four targets is thought to be not demanding enough or to give enough scope, more than six is likely to spread priority actions too thinly and to run the risk of making them too difficult to attain. Goals and targets do not have to be major aspects of a person's work; indeed some may appear to be fairly small things which could have an important effect on a person's overall performance.

Case Study 12.7:   *Exemplar*
GOALS AND TARGETS FOR MARTIN JARVIS

As a result of an appraisal interview with Vivienne Michael, Head of the Social Science faculty at Bestwick Park, these were the goals and targets agreed for Martin Jarvis, the Second in the History department.

Goal 1

To continue to develop particular management skills and expertise in preparation for taking on a Head of Department role in the future.

Targets
1 To learn to do the stationery and resources orders for the History department, and to take this responsibility on in the Spring Term, including leading department meeting discussions on how money should be spent.
2 To improve personal time management, and particularly to make more productive use of free periods in school time.

Goal 2

To continue to contribute to the department's curriculum development programme.

Targets
1 To prepare work on two sections of the new A level syllabus which the department will be adopting next year, and to report

to the department on this work at the end of the Autumn and Spring terms.

2 To review and modify two pieces of GCSE coursework during the course of the year.

3 To work with lower school Humanities teachers to develop more pupil-centred teaching and learning strategies, both by setting a personal example to others and by taking responsibility for planning a departmental INSET session in the Autumn Term – as part of this work to attend an appropriate LEA INSET course.

If Martin is to achieve these goals he will need support from Vivienne or others. Vivienne has suggested that Martin attends an LEA INSET course; it may be that Martin should be guided towards contacting the appropriate adviser or advisory teacher who could help with some of the curriculum development targets. In terms of the management targets Vivienne will need to have one or more sessions with Martin on how the stationery and resource orders are done in the school. She will also want to take the opportunity during the year for some informal chats about how well Martin is getting on in relation to the time management target.

Case Study 12.8:   *Exemplar*
A SAMPLE REVIEW SCHEDULE

Bestwick Park School
PERSONAL REVIEW OF THE YEAR

Use these headings to help you review your work over the past year. Please give your thoughts to the person who will be conducting your appraisal interview at least a week before the interview date you have agreed. Feel free to make any other points not covered below.

The positive aspects of the past year

1 What aspects of your work have given you the most satisfaction?
2 Have any classes or pupils been particularly rewarding?
3 Has anyone on the staff been of particular help to you in your work over the year?
4 What inservice training have you undertaken during the year (including departmental and in-school INSET)?
5 Are there skills or expertise which you feel you have been able to use particularly effectively during the year?

The negative aspects of the past year

1 What parts of your job do you find the least rewarding? Are there any particular reasons for this?
2 Do you feel that you have not dealt satisfactorily with any particular classes or pupils?
3 Have you found any tasks especially difficult this year? Are there any particular reasons for this?
4 Which of your skills or areas of expertise do you feel have been most underused or under-valued during the year?
5 Which aspects of your work in the school as a whole do you think most need further development and strengthening?

Professional development needs

1 What do you think will need to be the school's or the department's priority areas during the coming year?
2 What aspects of your work in school do you think should be your priority areas next year?
3 What are your ideas for tackling your priority areas?

Case Study 12.9: *For*
AN APPRAISAL CYCLE PLAN *reflection*

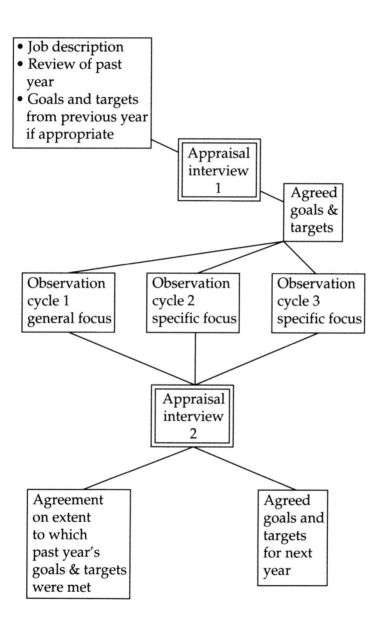

Counselling

Teaching is a high stress occupation, and most of us have problems from time to time. Often we can work at a problem and it goes away. Sometimes the problem is difficult to cope with, and it begins to affect our work, or home life, or both. Maybe it's a personal problem that is heightened by stress at work, perhaps a work problem that we cannot get out of our minds even at home, perhaps even something quite unimportant that we have got out of proportion because we are not feeling on top form at the time. Whatever the nature of the problem, or its cause, it can be that to talk it through with someone helps us to deal with it.

This is the basis of *counselling*. Counselling involves talking with someone for half an hour or so in a way that encourages them to talk, think through their situation or problem, and find possible solutions.

You may already have had experience of counselling, either in or out of school. As a middle manager you may find yourself in the position of wanting to counsel a member of your team. This may be something that is initiated by you when you can see that someone is upset or unusually tense, or it may be that someone in your team comes to you with a problem.

Counselling, if it is to be effective, has to be handled carefully and with sensitivity. In this section we cannot do more than outline some approaches to counselling, based on the ideas in a Video Arts film called *Can You Spare a Moment?*. If you are interested in counselling you might well start by getting hold of the film and its accompanying booklet.

There are two important points to note right at the start:

1 If you know that you are someone who is not cut out to do sensitive work like counselling, don't try – pass the person on to someone else who really is in a position to counsel.
2 When you counsel someone in your team you have to suspend your professional authority persona for the duration. A counselling interview is very different from other types of interviews you do in your professional capacity – appraisal or disciplinary interviews, for example – they must not be confused.

Some steps in counselling

Setting up the interview

People rarely advertise their problems, indeed, they often try to conceal them. One of your jobs as a team leader is to know your team well, and to be sensitive to the possibility of problems. So your first step is to be sensitive to the need. Often the key to the existence of a problem may lie in a colleague's altered behaviour.

Once you think that there may be a real need for a counselling session (and do not go searching for them, seeing problems where they do not exist)! you have to create the right opportunity to offer counselling. Half an hour to an hour should be enough time – any longer and the session may become protracted and purposeless. Counselling only works in a private, unhurried and undisturbed setting. It is up to you to create these conditions.

Encouraging people to talk

Once you have set up a counselling session, your next need is for the person to open up and talk about their problem. Of course, you cannot force them to talk; if they really do not want to, then simply let the opportunity slip by. However, they may just be having difficulty in getting started, and if so there are a number of techniques to encourage people to talk.

1 Offer reassurance, so that the person knows you are not disapproving or critical, eg *I can quite see why that's getting you down . . . Yes, I do understand . . .*
2 Be non-threatening if you have initiated the session, by saying something like: *I thought it might be helpful if we had a chat . . . You don't seem very happy at the moment, can I help?*
3 Ask open-ended questions that make it easier for the person to open up, such as, *How do you feel about that? When do you tend to get most angry? Who bothers you most? Where are you living now?*
4 Make the setting relaxed by sitting at a 90° angle to the person, or next to them – never opposite or across a desk.
5 Give your undivided attention – show that you are giving the person your full attention and maintain eye contact.
6 Listen carefully and demonstrate that you are hearing by rephrasing and summarising, for example, *So you are saying that . . . Let me just see if I have got that right . . .*

7   Don't say too much yourself, and encourage the person to talk
    by making 'listening' noises such as *uh huh* and *hummmm.*

Your behaviour is the key to successful counselling. Do not try
to give immediate answers – your aim is to encourage the person
to talk, and so your behaviour must be encouraging.

Helping people think through their problems
Having discovered what the problem is, the next step in
counselling is to help the person to accept responsibility for their
own problem, and to work out their own solution. It is their
problem, and in the end they have to solve it. Do not offer ready
made solutions – giving *your solution* to *their problem* is unlikely to
help, so resist the temptation.
    Your aim must be to be friendly and encouraging, and above all
neutral. As well as the encouraging behaviours outlined in the
previous section, you can use other approaches such as:

1   Admit your own fallibility in an honest, open way: *I've often
    made the same mistake . . . I must admit, I find that difficult too
    . . .*
2   Be non-judgemental – offer relevant advice, but do not express
    your views or criticisms: *We could give you some extra time for
    that . . . I think Mr Jones is aware of that . . .*
3   Ask questions to solicit ideas, and establish alternative ways to
    solve the problem, eg *So what do you think the options are? How
    can you avoid getting into that difficulty? How can you improve the
    situation?*
4   If you have to make suggestions, offer them as tentative
    questions, such as *How about doing so and so? I suppose one
    option would be . . .*

The main point to remember is to keep asking open-ended
questions, as this will help the person to think through to their
own solutions.

Letting people find their own solution
The final stage of a counselling session is to try and arrive at a
solution to the problem. But remember, your aim is for the person
to arrive at their own solution – it may not be the one you would
favour. Once they have reached this point:

1 Accept their solution even if you have misgivings. Your aim is to help and encourage, so be careful to support any solution that emerges from the session.
2 Agree an action plan, and if possible, a review date. This helps the person to be clear about what they are going to do, how they are going to do it, and by when.
3 Make it clear that you are always happy to talk to them again, not just for the review, if you have arranged one, but in the event of any further problems developing.

After the session
Because during the session you suspended any professional authority relationship you had with the person you were counselling, you need to be careful about your behaviour afterwards. Let things get back to normal as quickly as possible, and resist the temptation to check too obviously on progress. Your aim is to remain supportive in a low key way. The occasional 'caring' enquiry is fine, but do not put pressure on the person.

Finally, never betray confidences. The counselling session was private, and you suspended your professional persona for the duration – so no notes, or memos – or the person will never trust you again. The only exception to this is if, when drawing up the action plan, the person invited you to do something to help, or to bring other people into the process or knowledge of the problem.

Case Study 12.10:   *For action*
COUNSELLING HELEN TREVOR

From a conversation between Yvonne Perkins, Deputy Head, and Helen Trevor, Head of Chemistry.

I can't help noticing that you have been absent recently so much more than ever before, and that you simply don't seem to be as involved in things as you used to be. You were always my model of the conscientious member of staff. Is something wrong?

It transpires that Helen still resents the appointment of Simon Tucker as Head of the Science Faculty, and that she intensely dislikes the proposed changes to the Lower School science syllabus. Helen also feels threatened by some of the changes introduced by the new Head. Helen sums up her feelings by saying 'It's like being in a different school nowadays.'

1 *If you were in Yvonne Perkins' position, how would you approach counselling Helen Trevor?*
2 *What possible steps might you want to guide Helen towards taking?*
3 *What role might Simon Tucker, Helen's Head of Faculty, take in this matter, if any?*

Case Study 12.11: *For action*
COUNSELLING A STRESSED PROBATIONER

It is the end of the school day towards the end of the Christmas Term. You are on your way to a Head of Department meeting. On your way you pop into one of the department classrooms to pick up something. Sitting alone in the room is Peter, your probationary teacher, head in his hands, looking very down in the dumps. Peter has worked hard during his first term, and is proving to have the makings of a good teacher, although he has had some difficulties with discipline with his GCSE classes. At a recent parents' evening Peter had a hard time with a parent about the ways he was marking a pupil's work, although this is something you thought had been sorted out to everyone's satisaction.

'*Hello Peter, are you feeling alright?*'
'*Yes fine thanks, no problems.*'
'*Had a hard day?*'
'*Not too bad, well, pretty awful actually.*'

1 *What would you do then and there – bearing in mind that you are on your way to a meeting?*
2 *What further actions would you want to take at any other times?*

Chapter 13
Managing Change

As a manager you will be involved in dealing with problems and making decisions all the time. Many of your decisions will result in changes or modifications to the way you and your team operate. Most of the changes we make are fairly small scale. Every once in a while, however, you will find yourself in the position of having to manage a major change. Some examples of major changes controlled at middle management level might include:

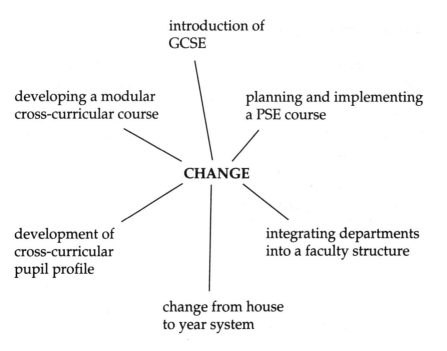

introduction of
GCSE

developing a modular
cross-curricular course

planning and implementing
a PSE course

CHANGE

development of
cross-curricular
pupil profile

integrating departments
into a faculty structure

change from house
to year system

Managing a major change like one of these will be one of the most demanding management tasks you will have to face. Moreover, because you are a middle manager in a school, you are unlikely to have either the time or the resources that would be available to your counterparts in industry.

One of the great temptations is to become too involved in details too quickly.

We all agree that we want to introduce a new modular Design and Technology course in the Lower School. Alright, why don't I produce a module on Food Technology; Mike, you have a go at a Craft Design module; and Vicki, you do one on Music Technology or something like that. OK?

Whoa! Slow down! It's good to see positive action, but this has jumped the gun by half a dozen crucial stages in the change management process. One of the recurring themes in this book has been that *time spent on planning always pays dividends later* – nowhere is this more true than in the management of a major change.

The change management model

In this chapter we are going to outline a Change Management Model, which you could use to guide you in the management of change. It is a variation of models used by a number of large commercial companies. In Rank Xerox, for example, it is accepted practice from board level down to use the ideas and techniques of the change management model to structure the planning process.

The change management model aims to provide a framework for planning and decision making. The key element of the model is that the planning process needs to follow certain stages. In this chapter we begin by outlining the model. Then we discuss some of the strategies and techniques you could use during the various stages of planning. Finally, we link the stages of the model, and the strategies we discuss, to a single case study of a curriculum change in a secondary school.

A last point before you set out on any major change, it is well worth recalling Murphy's Laws!

NOTHING IS AS SIMPLE AS IT SEEMS
EVERYTHING TAKES LONGER THAN YOU THINK
IF ANYTHING CAN GO WRONG - IT WILL

Change management

Stage 1: Prioritising
What are your major task priorities?
How do these tasks link with other things going on in school?
What timescale is involved in your priority tasks?
Which task needs doing most urgently?

Stage 2: Clarifying
What is the hoped-for outcome of this change?
What specific **objectives** must you set to achieve this outcome?
What is the main **target group** for the change?
Which other groups will be affected by any of your actions?
Who needs to be involved in decision making and action?

Stage 3: Creating
Identify your potential resources – what factors will help you gain your objectives?
What factors may **hinder** you in gaining your objectives?
Generate alternatives – what are **all** your possible courses of action?
Which courses of action are the most viable?
How should the best alternative be selected?

Stage 4: Formulating
At this planning stage you should consider questions such as:
Resourcing – How will this change be resourced? Time? Cost? People?
Influencing – Who has got to be won over? How?
Acting/delegating – What specific actions do you need to take? Who should be responsible for specific actions?
Prioritising – What is your timetable for action? Which are the priority actions? How do any actions mesh with your existing commitments?

Stage 5: Implementing
Is the planning stage now complete?
Are the targets and timetable clear, understood, and realistic?
Commitment – how can you gain and maintain the commitment of all the people involved in the change?
Communication – is your plan visible, and have your intentions been communicated to everyone who is affected?
How will communications be maintained while your actions continue?
Monitoring/control – how will your actions be co-ordinated and monitored, and by whom?

Stage 6: Reviewing
The reviewing process will take place both during the change, and after the change has been implemented.
Targets – are the targets for your actions at each stage clear and unambiguous?
How are you going to review your progress against the agreed targets?
Evaluation – how are you going to evaluate the impact of the change?
Who is the best person to make an objective evaluation?
How can your experience best be made available to others?

Case Study 13.1

Grafton School is a mixed 12–16 comprehensive with about 700 pupils on roll. In the past the school has had a reputation for providing a good, rather traditional, education in a friendly, caring atmosphere.

Grafton had a new Head a couple of years ago, and he has been making some changes to the curriculum of the school. One of the school's difficulties is that it faces a decline in pupil numbers, although the effects of this are not severe because the school always manages to attract a considerable number of pupils from outside its catchment area. In the light of falling rolls, the Head has begun to speak of 'some rationalisation of the curriculum' being necessary.

Traditionally the curriculum in the school has been organised along single subject lines, with many departments working very much on their own. In the last year the school has introduced a cross-curricular Information Technology initiative, and a new Business Studies course in the 4th and 5th years. The Head has made it clear that he is looking for further development of cross-curricular links, and for departments to work more closely together. To this end he has begun to reorganise departments into faculties.

One of the new faculties is Humanities, which covers the subject areas of History, Geography and RE. Although the humanities are still taught as single subjects all the way through the school, teaching is done in a Humanities block. The Humanities staff get on well together, and the subjects are popular when pupils opt in the 4th year. When the faculty was created the Head of History took on the Faculty Co-ordinator role. The faculty staff are:

Sarah   Faculty Co-ordinator and Head of History
Carol   Head of Geography
Bill   In charge of RE and teaches some Geography
Joan   History
Steve   English, but teaches some Humanities

The process of change illustrated in this case study was initiated by a discussion between the Head and Sarah, the Head of Faculty. The Head wanted Sarah to look at ways to improve the links between the Humanities departmental syllabuses, and floated the possibility of developing some integrated courses – although he was deliberately somewhat vague about this idea. They talked about the possible impact TVEI would have on the 4th and 5th year curriculum when the school went into the scheme in a year's time. They discussed the National Curriculum proposals, but agreed that there was little guidance as yet for the Humanities.

As it happens, shortly after her discussion with the Head, Sarah spent three days on a management course. She decided to try and use the Change Management Model when it came to planning change in the faculty back at school. She outlined the ideas in the model to the other members of the faculty, and with some reservations they agreed to try it out.

Prioritising

At any one time a team is likely to be faced by having to make a number of changes, and at no time more so than in the educational climate of today. Trying to do too much at once will almost certainly be counterproductive, so you will need to establish your priorities. Decide on the most important task, and focus your energies on that – tackle less but do it better.

This is how the Humanities team at Grafton tackled their prioritising.

Sarah arranged for the whole of the next weekly faculty meeting to be devoted to just this task – establishing their priority for action.

The meeting started with Sarah summarising again her conversation with the Head. She reported that the Head had hinted strongly about doing something in the 4th/5th years, but that he had not been specific. It was pointed out that the Science faculty was going to introduce a modular balanced science course in the 4th year next September.

Sarah suggested that they ignore the Head's hint for the moment, and that everyone should suggest possible priorities for action – being as partisan as they liked! The team suggested the following ideas:

- More Information Technology in Humanities courses
- A new integrated Humanities course in the lower school
- Links with English and Drama in the lower school courses
- Developing more fieldwork and work in the local area
- Changes to 4/5th year courses to integrate or link them

After discussion it was generally agreed that the Head was looking for a fairly substantial change, which meant doing something to either the Lower School or the Upper School courses. They decided to list the possible pros and cons of tackling each, and to give each point a double plus-to-double minus rating.

The result of this was a clear indication that the Lower School courses offered a more attractive proposition, and a stronger priority for action.

Lower School course		Upper School course	
+	Some courses have not changed much for some time	− −	Have already made major changes with introduction of GCSE
+ +	Need to make changes anyhow to bring in line with GCSE	+	Head seems to want it
− ?	Would involve more pupils and more teachers	+	May help Humanities to be more involved with TVEI
+ +	Easier to make changes in non-exam courses	−	How would parents/pupils react to changes in exam courses?
−	Head may not want it	−	Recently spent money on new GCSE resources – would that be wasted?
		+	Would link to changes in Science and Business Studies

Sarah agreed to speak to the Curriculum Deputy, to outline their thinking and obtain clearance to go ahead with some preliminary planning. The Deputy was enthusiastic, supported their reasoning, and agreed to brief (and persuade) the Head.

Clarifying

This is a crucial stage in the planning process, which people often miss out. It is also a stage which is harder than one might think!

Your first aim is to sort out exactly what you want, and need, to get out of the change you are planning, without tying yourselves down to details of actual schemes as yet. If you commit yourselves to something that is too precise at this stage you may close down possibilities too soon. You are trying to establish a goal towards which to plan. Only when you are clear about what your overall goal is going to be, can you begin to think about the various ways of achieving it.

Your second aim is to be clear about exactly who the change is for. Who is the *primary target group* – the main users of the change? Which group is the *target end user* – the people for whom the change is ultimately made? Which other people are affected by the change, and who needs to be involved, consulted or informed?

The Grafton Humanities team, like many people, did not find this stage easy. Predicting possible difficulties, Sarah had taken the precaution of inviting the subject adviser to the meeting.

Some of the initial efforts at clarifying the 'hoped for outcome' were rejected as being too specific. These included an integrated Humanities scheme involving History, Geography and RE; and a modular Humanities scheme in the Lower School.

This is the clarification that the team agreed on:

Hoped-for outcome
The successful introduction of a new Humanities syllabus in the Lower School, which meets these objectives:

1   Makes clear links between History, Geography and RE elements, and where possible includes other cross-curricular elements
2   Prepares pupils for their chosen GCSE courses in Humanities subjects
3   Includes a range of pupil-centred approaches to teaching and learning

The main target group is the pupils, as whatever we develop must be in the interests of improved learning for pupils.

Other groups involved in decision making: Curriculum Deputy (timetabling etc), Head (resources etc), possibly the adviser (resources, advice etc). Groups who need to be informed/consulted: parents, other Heads of Faculty/Depts.

Creating

Once you have clarified what you want to achieve through the process of change, the next stage involves thinking through *all* the possible approaches you could take.

Your aim is to be *creative* – to generate as many ideas about possible approaches as you can, even if at first sight some seem a bit impractical! In this way you are encouraging *lateral thinking*; it is remarkable how often being creative throws up good ideas that might otherwise never have emerged into the light of day.

To be creative it is best to work in a group, under relaxed conditions. Here are some approaches your team could take.

Brainstorming

1 Write your goal/hoped-for outcome at the top of a flipchart or on the board – so that everyone can see it.
2 Ask everyone in the team to quickly suggest ideas that could move you towards your goal – stress that any ideas, however zany, are acceptable.
3 One person notes the ideas on the flipchart or board as they are given. Do not discuss details at this stage – just accept any idea that is put forward.
4 Keep the brainstorming going as long as ideas keep coming – if necessary throw in a few provocative ideas yourself just to stir things up a bit.

Selecting possibilities

Your objective now is to select the best ideas from the brainstorm list – some of the suggestions can usually be rejected pretty quickly!

1 Ask the team to select the three or four most promising ideas – if in doubt or disagreement over anything, keep the idea in at this stage.
2 Discuss the possible ideas in more detail – try asking the team to think of three strong points and three weak points about each selected idea.
3 Can you make a final selection on the basis of what you have just done? If there is strong agreement, go for a decision. Or do you need time for further research/consultation/discussion? If you need more time – set out a timetable for decision making, and clarify who is going to do what in the meantime.

This is what the Grafton Humanities team produced in their brainstorming:

SINGLE SUBJECT MODULES WITH CONTENT LINKS

EVERYBODY WHAT THEY DO LIKE!

CORE OPTION + MODULES

GEOG ONE YEAR
HISTORY THE NEXT

RE SEPARATE

FULLY INTEGRATED COURSE

INTEGRATE OR ENGLISH SCIENCE WITH

CARRY ON AS BEFORE

AN INFORMATION
TECH INTEGRATED
MODULE

GO IN WITH BUSINESS
STUDIES-TO FORM A
MEGA - FACULTY

COMBINATION OF SINGLE SUBJECT + INTEGRATED MODULES

CALL OURSELVES
SOCIAL SCIENCE

The team identified three ideas for further discussion.

1 Single subject modules with content links
2 Integrated content throughout
3 Combination of subject and integrated modules

Two other ideas were identified as having potential, and they were noted for further consideration at a later date.

4 An Information Technology based module
5 English and Drama input integrated with course (Steve was delegated to sound out the Head of English on this idea)

Discussion of the advantages and disadvantages of the three main ideas produced strong support for the 'combined module' option, with one person arguing for the 'single subject' option.

After further discussion it was agreed to move on the 'combined module' option as this most effectively met the objectives and targets.

- single subject modules allow scope for GCSE subject preparation
- integrated modules allow more scope for cross-curricular work
- the combination allows wide scope to develop pupil-centred approaches to teaching and learning
- the primary target group – themselves – were most positive about this option, while it also met the needs of pupils as end users

---

Another of your aims in the creative stage is to identify possible resources that will help you achieve your hoped for outcome. 'Resources' in this context means anything that you could use to help you – people, ideas, time, physical resources, influence. One approach to identifying both positive and negative resources is a simple technique called 'force field analysis'.

Like brainstorming, force field analysis is best done in a group, using a large sheet of paper or the board so that people can see ideas being developed.

Force field analysis
1 Identify the 'ideal solution' you want to move towards, and write this at the top of the sheet.
2 Identify any possible resource which could help move towards your ideal result. These are your *driving forces*. Write these on the driving force side of your sheet. You do not need to go into too much detail at this stage – indeed you might brainstorm to generate a wide range of ideas on driving forces.
3 Now go through a similar process to identify all the possible *resisting forces*, which are the elements which could work against your achieving the change towards your ideal situation.
4 Once you have identified all possible driving and resisting forces, go back to analyse them in more detail. Try to assess the relative importance of each force – make the length or the width of each line roughly proportional to the strength of the force.

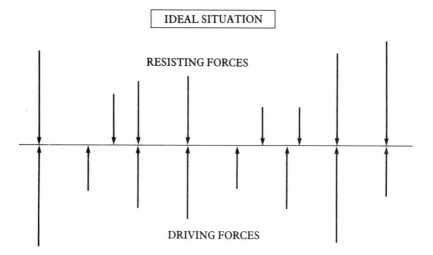

5   What are the key driving forces? What can you plan to do to maximise their effect?
6   What are the key resisting forces? How can you plan to minimise or eliminate their effects?

The force field analysis produced by the Grafton Humanities team is shown opposite.

Notice that some of the forces appear on both sides, because they are potential driving forces if they can be harnessed – but also have the potential to be resistances. One such example is the Head, whose support was seen as crucial for achieving success, but who could block elements of the scheme if he was not won over.

What did their force field analysis show the team?

They felt that nothing particularly startling had emerged, but that it had been very positive to get this sort of thinking out into the open, as it would help to focus their thoughts in the formulating and implementing stages. In the next case study section, you can see how the team tried to maximise their driving forces, and minimise potential resisting forces.

IDEAL
SITUATION = Successful introduction of a modular course with subject
& integrated modules.

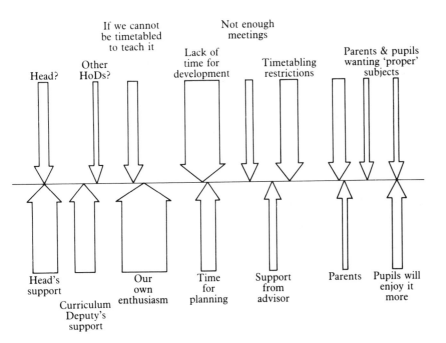

If we cannot
be timetabled
to teach it

Not enough
meetings

Lack of
time for
development

Other
HoDs?

Head?

Timetabling
restrictions

Parents & pupils
wanting 'proper'
subjects

Head's
support

Our
own
enthusiasm

Time
for
planning

Support
from
advisor

Parents

Pupils will
enjoy it
more

Curriculum
Deputy's
support

DRIVING FORCES

Formulation and implementation

Having completed the first three clarification/creation stages you should now be in a good position to plan a strategy for making your change.

Although the stages of 'formulation' and 'implementation' are outlined as separate stages in the Change Management Model, you may find that they overlap to some extent. The key point is to keep all your clarification work to the forefront of your minds as you formulate and implement.

- How are you planning to involve those people who can help drive you towards your goal?
- How are you planning to win over people who might be resisting forces?
- How are you planning to gain the time or money you have identified as being necessary for success?
- How are you planning to keep your activities visible?
- What are your priorities and deadlines for work that needs to be done?

Critical path analysis
To keep a check on deadlines you could do a simple *critical path analysis*. This involves agreeing your timetable for action, and listing on it all the deadlines and the various periods for tasks you have to complete. This helps you to plan ahead to meet deadlines, and to allow enough time for activities that may be lengthy.

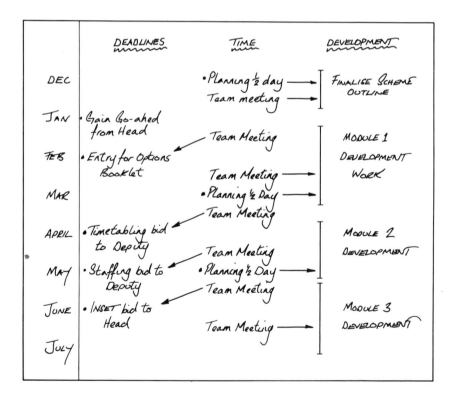

By this stage the Grafton Humanities team were beginning detailed planning and development work, and it would be inappropriate to report in detail on their activities. Their critical path is outlined, and some key planning points relating to their force field analysis are reported.

- **Time** was seen as critical. They agreed to introduce the scheme with the entry year next September. To gain the necessary planning time they put in a bid to the Head for supply cover to release all the faculty – 1 full day, and 3 half days spread over the rest of the development year. The Head was able to do this by splitting the cost of supply with the adviser – an advantage in having involved her early in the process.
- The active support of the **Curriculum Deputy** and **Head** were seen as critical. It was agreed that draft plans etc would be given to both, and that Sarah would be responsible for keeping both fully briefed.

  The Curriculum Deputy was the key to timetabling. Early on Sarah negotiated 5 periods for entry year Humanities, with all classes blocked at the same time, and with one whole afternoon given over to the course. This was seen as an important element in being able to develop more active, pupil-centred teaching and learning strategies. The Curriculum Deputy was also made aware of staffing needs, and while she could not commit herself so early, she did agree to try and meet their needs.

  In the event, although staffing needs were met (the development team were all timetabled to teach Humanities), it turned out impossible to block all the groups. However, without early negotiation the situation would almost certainly have been less favourable.

  The Head was the key to resources. Planning time had already been negotiated, and early discussions with the Head did allow the team to make use of some money that was left at the end of the financial year. The Head was able to make some additional funds available for the introduction year, although not as much as the team wanted!
- **Parents and pupils** – the team decided to brief the Head of

Lower School, so that he was aware of developments, and would be in a position to explain the scheme on his visits to feeder primary schools. Early decision making meant that the team was in a position to outline and explain the scheme fully in the school's booklet to new parents.

- **Other staff** had been briefed in a short session at the start of a regular staff meeting. Steve had been delegated to keep the Head of English fully briefed, and in the event he proved very useful in providing some resources and INSET on using drama techniques.

Reviewing

You will want to build into your planning a procedure for monitoring and reviewing your progress towards implementing a major change. You will also need to determine right from the outset how to evaluate the impact of the change and who will do so.

Your evaluation will assess to what extent your implementation of the change has achieved the goal you established at the start of the process. For a curriculum change the key question is likely to be:

- What impact has been made on the quality of the learning experience of the pupils?

Other evaluation elements might include:

- impact on staff workload
- quality of resources
- costs – both time and money.

It is often the case that the team which has planned and carried out a major change find that they are too close to events to be able to make a suitably detached, objective evaluation. It is common practice in research projects for the project team to appoint an external evaluator, whose job it is to contribute to both formative evaluation during the project, and to make a summative evaluation at the end; the external evaluator is thus both involved with the project, yet at the same time stands detached from day-to-day decision making.

The Grafton Humanities team built in procedures for monitoring and evaluation.

1 *Monitoring*
   Each member of the team was responsible for monitoring progress on one module. This involved chasing people up for deadlines; ensuring that resource material was produced; reviewing the assessments used.

2 *Evaluation*
   The adviser was used as a form of external evaluator. She commented on planning, module outlines and teaching materials, and observed a number of lessons (feeding back observations to both individual teachers and the team).

3 *Feedback from pupils*
   It was agreed right from the start that the team would involve pupils in the review process. A pro forma was used to invite pupils to comment at the end of each module – on what they had enjoyed most and least, on what they felt was their best work, on any changes they would like to see etc.

Chapter 14
Performance Evaluation

One of the recurring themes of this book has been that effective management requires three distinct activities.

1 WHAT?/WHY? – Establishing priorities. Setting objectives.
2 HOW? – Formulating. Implementing.
3 HOW WELL? Reviewing. Evaluating.

One of the criticisms that has been levelled at schools and the teaching profession in recent years is that they are not rigorous enough in the way they evaluate performance – their own performance as teachers and managers. Words like 'complacent' and 'self-satisfied' have been bandied about.

In our experience much of this criticism is unfair. The teachers and managers in most schools and departments really do care about their performance, and about the quality of education they are providing for pupils. However, that said, there is no doubt that there is more than a grain of truth in the criticisms – the process of performance evaluation in education, no matter how well intentioned, often lacks rigour.

One of the reasons for this is that, as people involved in education, we are all so closely involved in the process; we are so close to what is going on, and have so much 'professional capital' tied up in the venture, that it really is hard to be objective. This is the root of the difficulty.

Rigorous evaluation requires *objectivity*, and objectivity requires the use of *evidence* rather than an emotional response. We may know that we are working hard, we may believe sincerely that we are doing what is best for our pupils, we may feel strongly that things are going well, but those emotional responses, although very important, are not in themselves a basis for objective and rigorous performance evaluation.

It is easy enough to argue for objective performance evaluation, the difficulty lies in how to do it! The real problem lies in what we accept as evidence of good performance. In other words, what do we mean by 'good education', and what is the 'evidence' by which we can evaluate whether or not it is being provided?

Performance indicators

There is much talk in education at the moment of *performance indicators*. We would argue that some of it is uninformed and simplistic, but that the concept of performance indicators can be a useful one in performance evaluation.

A performance indicator:

- focuses on a single pre-determined element of a wider, more diffuse process
- outlines a way in which performance in this single element can be measured or objectively assessed
- takes this measurement as evidence of the overall standard of performance in the wider, more diffuse process as a whole.

Schools and departments have always used some performance indicators, for example:

1 *The numbers of pupils choosing a subject in the 4th year.* Because this is something measurable it is often taken as a performance indicator of the quality of teaching/educational experience in the lower school.
2 *Pupils' achievements in public examinations.* This is a commonly-used performance indicator of the quality and effectiveness of subject teaching in the school.
3 *The appearance of pupils, particularly with respect to school uniform.* This is often used as a performance indicator of school 'ethos'.
4 *The number of clubs, societies and out of school activities.* This is used as a performance indicator of the quality of extra-curricular provision in a school.

All of the above performance indicators, and many more, are useful. Indeed they are elements, it can be argued, that a school needs to be concerned with. The danger lies in uncritical or insensitive use of performance indicators. They need to be evaluated in the light of questions like the following:

- What is the performance indicator actually measuring?
- Is the use of the performance indicator set in its proper context?
- Is evidence provided by a performance indicator supported by other, perhaps less measurable or more subjective, criteria?

Take the first performance indicator outlined above – option choices – which is commonly used at department level. This does provide a useful, easily measurable guide to department performance in the lower school years; a department which consistently has few pupils opting for its courses at GCSE should have cause for concern. But, on the other hand, a substantial number of pupils opting may not in itself be an indicator of high quality provision in the lower school, for a number of reasons.

- The subject may be viewed as an 'easy option'.
- Numbers opting may depend on the strong personality of just one or two lower school teachers.
- Pressure, perhaps unintentional, may be put on pupils to opt for that subject.
- The lower school teaching may be highly didactic, which many pupils find satisfying and 'performance geared'.
- Numbers opting may reflect the way the option system is organised.
- High numbers opting may reflect 'lesser of two evils' thinking.

In this instance, we are arguing that, while a measurable performance indicator is a useful evaluation tool, it is not in itself evidence of achieving your real aim – the provision of high quality educational experience for the pupils you teach. The performance indicator should be used, but used in context, and used with other means of evaluating your performance against all the aims and objectives you have established.

Evaluating your performance

In the remainder of this chapter we outline some examples of performance evaluation checklists and approaches, geared to

- evaluating department or team performance
- evaluating management performance
- evaluating personal performance

None of the approaches use only performance indicators, but some of them do attempt to focus on a limited number of performance criteria.

In the final analysis the effectiveness of any performance evaluation will depend on the objectivity with which it is applied. Objectivity does not necessarily mean 'from the outside', although to include some form of external evaluation can be very effective. Whatever process you develop it is likely to include some 'objective' indicators (including some that are easily measurable) and some 'subjective' assessments.

In evaluating your own performance, either as teacher or manager, and the performance of the team you manage, the key to being effective is to be *open*. This involves:

- openness in accepting and analysing positive criticism
- having an open mind to suggestions and alternatives
- opening the process to all people who can make a positive contribution

---

Case Study 14.1:   *For*
EVALUATING THE QUALITY OF TEACHING   *reflection*
AND LEARNING

These ideas on evaluation criteria come from a group of teachers from different schools working together on an INSET course.

1 Quality of the learning environment

- appearance of the room;
- displays on wall

To what extent could you use these words . . .?

interesting   well-organised   clean and tidy
businesslike   uncluttered

2 Quality of relationships

- between pupils and teacher
- among pupils
- among teachers

To what extent are these qualities evident . . .?

courtesy   respect   humour   sensitivity
encouragement

3 Quality of teaching and learning

- Learning experience
- Teaching strategies

To what extent do these conditions exist . . .?

- full involvement
- taking responsibility
- enthusiasm
- challenge

- clarity of purpose
- relaxed control
- enthusiasm
- differentiation

Case Study 14.2:   *For*
EVALUATING YOURSELF AS A MANAGER   *reflection*

This document was produced, as a first draft, by a group of teachers and advisers, whose brief was to outline ways in which the effectiveness of middle management in a school could be monitored and evaluated.

Quality of leadership
Middle management in secondary schools

Elements
In any assessment of leadership quality, in whatever educational situation, the group suggested that there are three key elements. These elements are distinctive but not discrete.

Indicators
The group considered possible positive indicators which would point towards an effective leadership by a middle manager. The aim was to identify indicators that really could be identified during a school review exercise.

The group considered that it could be counter-productive to generate too many indicators, and aimed to suggest about six for each element of leadership quality.

People management

- Strong team identity – Is there a clear sense among people of belonging to a team?
- Clear communications up and down – Are information and ideas properly communicated among all team members?
- Shared aims and objectives within the team – Are all team members clearly aware of team tasks/aims/objectives?
- Open discussion within the team – Can team members voice differences of opinion without disturbing the effectiveness of the team?
- Individual expertise is valued – Are the particular skills/expertise/qualities of team members recognised and used? Are weaknesses minimised?
- High morale – Is there a positive attitude among all team members in relation to the team tasks?
- Team visibility – Does the team have a clear and recognised identity amongst people who are not in the team itself?

Task management

1 Aims and objectives – Are the team aims and objectives clearly defined in writing? Are these aims and objectives derived from school aims?

2 Decision making – Is the process of decision making in the team effective? Is there evidence that decision-making involves all team members?

3 Review and evaluation – Are there clearly defined processes whereby the team's work and aims/objectives are reviewed and evaluated?

4 Task achievement – Is there evidence that previously defined team tasks have been taken through to a successful conclusion?

5 Deployment of resources – Is there evidence that the team's resources (time, space, money) are effectively deployed? Are resources fairly deployed within the team?

6 Strategic planning – Is there a means by which the team undertakes long-term planning?

7 Team meetings – Is there a pattern of properly organised meetings, formal or informal as appropriate, with agenda and minutes where necessary?

Personal qualities
These would be some of the personal qualities and expertise shown by an effective middle manager.

1 Positive attitude
2 Self-confidence
3 Sensitivity to others
4 Ability to delegate
5 Broad educational perspective
6 Classroom competence
7 Curriculum/pastoral expertise

A Short Reading List for Middle Managers

Some management books end with half a dozen pages of references and suggestions for further reading. Somehow we do not feel that is going to be useful for busy middle managers!

We have selected a dozen books, series or kits on management which we have found useful in one way or another. We hope that you will find in at least some of them ideas and material to further develop your own management skills and understanding.

General school management

1 *Management in Schools*
The Industrial Society (1983)
A series of short (25 pages) booklets on topics including Leadership, Effective Use of Time, Teamwork in Schools. First published in 1983 this series provides a useful introduction to management. The series incorporates the ideas of John Adair (two of whose books are listed below).

2 *Effective School Management*
K. Everard and G. Morris (Harper, 1985)
Heavier going than the Industrial Society booklets, but a thoroughly good management book.

3 *Understanding Schools as Organisations*
C. Handy and R. Aitkin (Penguin, 1986)
This is a follow-up to *Taken for Granted? Understanding Schools as Organisations* which Charles Handy wrote in 1984 for the Schools Council's 'Purpose and Planning in Schools'

project. One of his aims was to investigate the differences between schools and business, and the book contains his ideas about organisational cultures. If you get interested you may want to read his more recent *The Gods of Management*, also published by Penguin.

4 *Developing Management in Schools*
K. Everard (Blackwell, 1986)
Geared more to senior management, but still an interesting and illuminating book to dip into. There are three sections – School Management Observed, Industrial Management Compared, and School Management Developed.

5 *Are You Managing?*
P. Stemp (Industrial Society, 1988)
This book was originally written for Allied Dunbar by their Personnel Director, Peter Stemp. It looks at what you need to do to be an effective manager, and at how to improve your practice. Remember that it is written primarily for an industrial audience.

Departmental management

6 *Management in School Science Departments*
Published jointly by British Gas and The Association for Science Education (ASE)
There are four kits in this series, each written by a team drawn from science teachers and industrial management trainers. Although geared particularly at science departments, most of the material has a wider application. Four useful and practical kits including notes, training ideas and materials, OHP masters and a tape. The four titles are Understanding Management Roles, Time Management, Staff Development – Selection and Appraisal, Meetings as Vehicles for Communication.

7 *Decisions in the Science Department – Organisation and Curriculum*
R. Hull and H. Adams (Schools Council/ASE, 1981)
Also geared particularly at science teachers, but with some wider application. A bit dated now, especially in light of the National Curriculum changes, but some good ideas on decision-making and on managing change in the department.

Team building and leadership

8 *Effective Team Building*
J. Adair (Gower, 1986)
John Adair is one of the most influential management trainers. This book develops in more depth some of the ideas we have used, and particularly the interlocking of team, task and individual needs in an effective team.

9 *The Skills of Leadership*
J. Adair (Wildwood House, 1984)
An interesting analysis of the nature of leadership in general, rather than in the educational context. Rather dated in places now, as the first version was published (difficult to believe) in 1934.

10 *Management Teams – Why They Succeed or Fail*
R. Belbin (Heinemann, 1981)
The definitive analysis of team characteristics and the role of individual team members. This fascinating and delightfully written book is based on years of research among course members at the Henley Management College. You could try your hand at Belbin's Self Perception Inventory, and discover your predominant team role characteristic.

Appraisal

11 *Teacher Appraisal in Practice*
Ed. S. Bunnell (Heinemann, 1987)
One of the books in the Heinemann 'Organisation in Schools' series. A drawback of the books in this series is that each chapter is written by a different person, and there is insufficient overview at times.

12 *The Appraisal Interview*
E. Hewton (The Open University, 1988)
A short and useful book on a theme that will be increasingly of concern to middle managers in schools. The book includes suggestions for workshop activities to develop appraisal interview skills.